Introduction

Sometimes a simple idea turns out to be a great idea. That's how it's been with *Quiltmaker's* **Patch Pals Collection**. We wondered if we could create pictorial quilts using squares and triangle-squares, and the answer was yes! When we started with a teddy bear, we could not have foreseen the fun this animal parade would become. *Beary Patch* was just a whimsical name choice, but it started us on a path of finding clever names for each quilt that followed. What a ball we've had brainstorming when it's time to christen each new project!

These 12 crib quilts originally appeared in *Quiltmaker's* 2011–2012 issues. The quilts are all the same size so that the borders are all interchangeable; see page 52 for a couple of options. Would you like to try your hand at coloring your own pal? We've included graph paper designs of each **Patch Pal** that you can color your way on pages 59–63. For more inspiration visit our Reader's Gallery on pages 53–56.

We hope you love these are much as we do, and that you'll find them to be great gifts for babies and kids of all ages.

Leisure Arts, Inc.
Little Rock, Arkansas

Patch Pals Collection

Quilts designed by Denise Starck

Edited by Paula Stoddard

Additional editing by Amy Rullkoetter

Designed by Ann Hardell

***Quiltmaker* Staff**

Editor-in-Chief: June Dudley

Art Director: Ian Davis

Creative Editor: Carolyn Beam

Associate Editors: Eileen Fowler, Paula Stoddard

Interactive Editor: Diane Volk Harris

Graphic Designer: Denise Starck

Editorial Assistant: Shayla Wolf

Photographer: Mellisa Karlin Mahoney

Quiltmaker®, ISSN 1047-1634, USPS 4416, is published bi-monthly by Creative Crafts Group, LLC; 741 Corporate Circle, Suite A; Golden, CO 80401; quiltmaker.com.

Library of Congress Control Number: 2013938847
Print edition ISBN: 978-1-4647-0863-3
Published by Leisure Arts, Inc., www.leisurearts.com.

Produced by the editors of *Quiltmaker* magazine for Leisure Arts, Inc., 5701 Ranch Drive, Little Rock, AR 72223-9633.

Contents

Purr Patch 8

Beary Patch 12

Quack Patch 16

Banana Patch 24

Prickly Patch 28

Peanut Patch 32

Pokey Patch 40

Polar Patch 44

Jingle Patch 48

Ruff Patch

Friendly pup makes a fetching quilt

Made by Peg Spradlin.

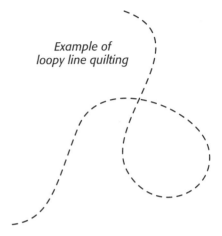

Example of loopy line quilting

materials

Crib: 40¼" x 50¾"

Assorted Light Blue Tone-on-Tones
½ yard *total* for background

Assorted Medium Brown Tone-on-Tones
⅛ yard *total* for ears and eyes

Assorted Cream Tone-on-Tones
1½ yards *total* for dog and border #2

Assorted Dark Brown and Black Tone-on-Tones
⅞ yard *total* for face, paw, tail and border #2

Assorted Medium Red Tone-on-Tones
⅛ yard *total* for bandana

Medium Red Tone-on-Tone
1 yard for border #1, cornerstones and binding

Backing 2¾ yards (with careful basting, 1 fabric width at 1⅝ yards will be sufficient)

Batting 45" x 59"

Tear-away stabilizer

cutting

▨ = cut in half diagonally
⊠ = cut in half twice diagonally

Assorted Light Blue Tone-on-Tones
15 squares 2⅝" x 2⅝" ▨ (A)
81 squares (B) 2¼" x 2¼"

Assorted Medium Brown Tone-on-Tones
5 squares 2⅝" x 2⅝" ▨ (A)
8 squares (B) 2¼" x 2¼"

Assorted Cream Tone-on-Tones
18 strips 2¼" x 20" for bands
17 squares 2⅝" x 2⅝" ▨ (A)
154 squares (B) 2¼" x 2¼"

Assorted Dark Brown and Black Tone-on-Tones
18 strips 2¼" x 20" for bands
6 squares 2⅝" x 2⅝" ▨ (A)
14 squares (B) 2¼" x 2¼"

Assorted Medium Red Tone-on-Tones
6 squares 2⅝" x 2⅝" ▨ (A)
9 squares (B) 2¼" x 2¼"

Medium Red Tone-on-Tone
for border #1
2 strips 2¼" x 37¼" for sides
2 strips 2¼" x 30¼" for top/bottom
6 strips 2¼" x 40" for binding
4 squares (C) 5¾" x 5¾"

1 Making the Quilt Center

Referring to the unit diagrams, pair the A's in the appropriate colors to make the unit 1's–8's as shown.

Unit 1
Make 6

Unit 2
Make 3

Unit 3
Make 6

Unit 4
Make 1

Unit 5
Make 16

Unit 6
Make 3

Unit 7
Make 9

Unit 8
Make 5

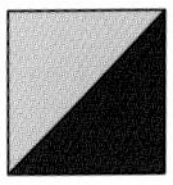

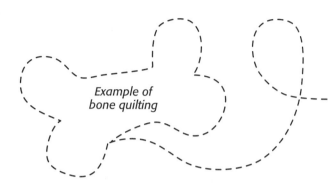

Example of bone quilting

Referring to the assembly diagram, join the B's and units to make the sections 1–6. Sew the sections together to make the quilt center.

With a tear-away stabilizer on the back, use dark thread and a machine satin stitch about ¼"-wide to embroider the dog's mouth as shown in the quilting placement diagram.

Machine Satin Stitch

2 Adding the Borders

To make the border #2 units, join strips as shown to make 6 band A's and 6 band B's. Cut each band in 2¼" increments to make 42 unit 9's and 38 unit 10's.

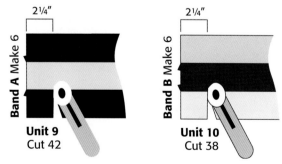

Band A Make 6	Band B Make 6
2¼"	2¼"
Unit 9 Cut 42	**Unit 10** Cut 38

Refer to the assembly diagram. For each border #2 side strip, join 12 unit 9's and 11 unit 10's as shown. For each border #2 top and bottom strip, join 9 unit 9's and 8 unit 10's as shown; add a red C to each end.

Matching centers and ends, sew the border #1 side strips to the quilt. Repeat to add the border #1 top and bottom strips. Add border #2 in the same way.

Quilting Placement

3 Quilting and Finishing

Beginning in the upper left-hand corner of the background and using the patchwork as a guide, mark a grid over the background as shown. Layer and baste together the backing, batting and quilt top.

Quilt the dog's body and border #1 in the ditch as shown. Quilt the eyebrows and eye patch in the ditch. Quilt parallel lines in the ears and bandana. Quilt circles over the eyes. Quilt the nose, whiskers and paws as shown. Meander quilt over the dog's body. Quilt the marked grid. Quilt a looping line in border #1. Quilt freeform loops, randomly adding bones in border #2. Bind the quilt. 🐾🐾

Section 1

Unit 9
Unit 10

C

Unit 9

Unit 10

Section 2

Section 3

Section 4

Section 5

Section 6

Assembly

Purr Patch

Take a catnap with a cuddly kitty

Made by Peg Spradlin.

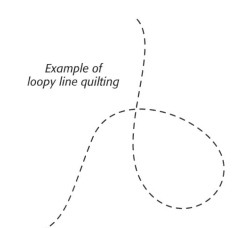

Example of loopy line quilting

materials

Crib: 40¼" x 50¾"

Assorted Light Green Tone-on-Tones
½ yard *total* for background
Assorted Orange Tone-on-Tones
1⅛ yards *total* for cat and border #2
Pink Tone-on-Tone
scraps for ears and nose
Assorted Black Tone-on-Tones
⅜ yard *total* for cat and border #2
Dark Green Tone-on-Tone
1 yard for eyes, border #1,
cornerstones and binding
White on White Print
scraps for cat's chest
Assorted Rust Tone-on-Tones
⅛ yard *total* for cat
Light Green Tone-on-Tone
⅝ yard for border #2
Backing 2¾ yards (with careful basting, 1 fabric width at 1⅝ yards will be
sufficient)
Batting 45" x 59"
Tear-away stabilizer

cutting

◨ = cut in half diagonally
⊠ = cut in half twice diagonally

Assorted Light Green Tone-on-Tones
14 squares 2⅝" x 2⅝" ◨ (A)
82 squares (B) 2¼" x 2¼"
Assorted Orange Tone-on-Tones
30 squares 2⅝" x 2⅝" ◨ (A) (there
will be 1 extra)
193 squares (B) 2¼" x 2¼"
Pink Tone-on-Tone
1 square 2⅝" x 2⅝" ◨ (A)
1 square (B) 2¼" x 2¼"
Assorted Black Tone-on-Tones
14 squares 2⅝" x 2⅝" ◨ (A)
44 squares (B) 2¼" x 2¼"
Dark Green Tone-on-Tone
for border #1
2 strips 2¼" x 37¼" for sides
2 strips 2¼" x 30¼" for top/bottom
6 strips 2¼" x 40" for binding
2 squares 2⅝" x 2⅝" ◨ (A)
4 squares (C) 5¾" x 5¾"

White on White Print
1 square 2⅝" x 2⅝" ◨ (A)
2 squares (B) 2¼" x 2¼"
Assorted Rust Tone-on-Tones
10 squares 2⅝" x 2⅝" ◨ (A) (there
will be 1 extra)
2 squares (B) 2¼" x 2¼"
Light Green Tone-on-Tone
for border #2
4 strips 2¼" x 40¾" for sides
4 strips 2¼" x 30¼" for top/bottom

1 Making the Quilt Center

Referring to the unit diagrams, pair the A's in the appropriate colors to make the unit 1's–8's as shown.

Unit 1
Make 16

Unit 2
Make 2

Unit 3
Make 19

Unit 4
Make 4

Unit 5
Make 9

Unit 6
Make 2

Unit 7
Make 16

Unit 8
Make 3

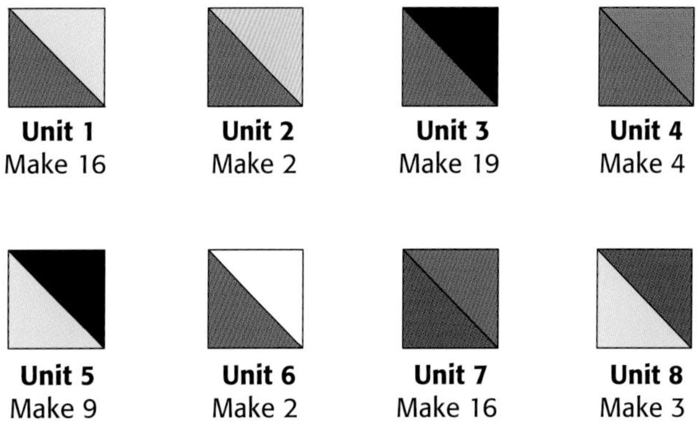

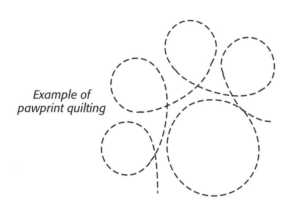

*Example of
pawprint quilting*

Quilting Placement

Referring to the assembly diagram, join the B's and units to make the sections 1–6. Sew the sections together to make the quilt center.

With a tear-away stabilizer on the back, use dark thread and a machine satin stitch about ¼" -wide to embroider the cat's mouth as shown on the quilting placement diagram.

Machine Satin Stitch

2 Adding the Borders

Refer to the assembly diagram. To make each border #2 side strip, join 12 black B's and 11 orange B's as shown. Matching centers and ends, sew a 2¼"x 40¾" light green strip along each side.

To make each border #2 top and bottom strip, join 9 black B's and 8 orange B's as shown. Matching centers and ends, sew a 2¼"x 30¼" light green strip along each side. Sew a dark green C to each end.

Matching centers and ends, sew the border #1 side strips to the quilt. Repeat to add the border #1 top and bottom strips. Add border #2 in the same way.

3 Quilting and Finishing

Beginning in the upper left-hand corner of the background and using the patchwork as a guide, mark a grid over the background as shown. Layer and baste together the backing, batting and quilt top.

Quilt the cat's body, facial features, chest and border #1 in the ditch as shown. Quilt the cat's eyes, nose, whiskers and paws as shown. Meander quilt over the cat's body. Quilt the marked grid. Quilt a looping line in border #1. Quilt freeform loops, randomly adding paw prints in border #2. Bind the quilt. 🐾🐾

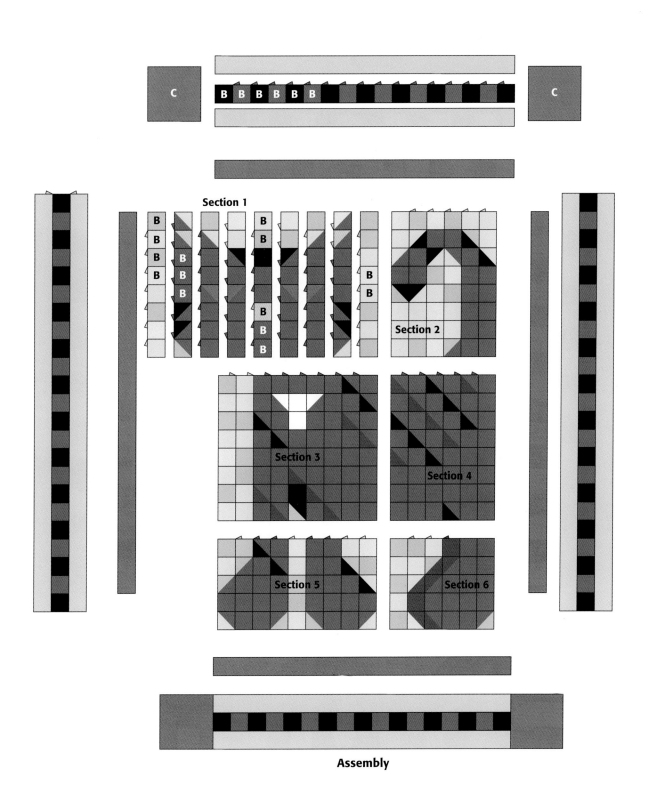

Section 1

Section 2

Section 3

Section 4

Section 5

Section 6

Assembly

Beary Patch

Curl up with this furry friend

Made by Peg Spradlin.

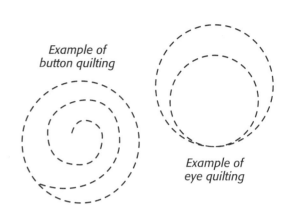

Example of button quilting

Example of eye quilting

materials

Crib: 40¼" x 50¾"

Assorted Cream Tone-on-Tones
1⅛ yards *total* for background and border

Assorted Dark Brown Tone-on-Tones
1⅜ yards *total* for bear body and border

Assorted Pink Tone-on-Tones
¼ yard *total* for bear accents

Black Tone-on-Tone
scraps for buttons and eyebrows

Assorted Medium Brown Tone-on-Tones
⅜ yard *total* for bear feet

Blue Tone-on-Tone
scrap for eyes

Pink Tone-on-Tone
⅝ yard for border #1 and corner-stones

Brown Tone-on-Tone
½ yard for binding

Backing 2¾ yards (with careful basting, 1 fabric width at 1⅝ yards will be sufficient)

Batting 45" x 59"

Tear-away stabilizer

cutting

☐ = cut in half diagonally
☒ = cut in half twice diagonally

Assorted Cream Tone-on-Tones
14 squares 2⅝" x 2⅝" ☐ (A)
1 square 3" x 3" ☒ (B) (there will be 2 extra)
103 squares (C) 2¼" x 2¼"
38 rectangles (D) 2¼" x 5¾"

Assorted Dark Brown Tone-on-Tones
16 squares 2⅝" x 2⅝" ☐ (A)
1 square 3" x 3" ☒ (B) (there will be 2 extra)
120 squares (C) 2¼" x 2¼"
42 rectangles (D) 2¼" x 5¾"

Assorted Pink Tone-on-Tones
7 squares 2⅝" x 2⅝" ☐ (A)
9 squares (C) 2¼" x 2¼"

Black Tone-on-Tone
1 square 2⅝" x 2⅝" ☐ (A)
3 squares (C) 2¼" x 2¼"

Assorted Medium Brown Tone-on-Tones
11 squares 2⅝" x 2⅝" ☐ (A)
28 squares (C) 2¼" x 2¼"

Blue Tone-on-Tone
2 squares (C) 2¼" x 2¼"

Pink Tone-on-Tone
for border #1
2 strips 2¼" x 37¼" for sides
2 strips 2¼" x 30¼" for top/bottom
4 squares (E) 5¾" x 5¾"

Brown Tone-on-Tone
6 strips 2¼" x 40" for binding

1 Making the Quilt Top

Referring to the unit diagrams, use A's and B's in the appropriate colors to make the unit 1's–8's as shown.

Unit 1
Make 16

Unit 2
Make 10

Unit 3
Make 2

Unit 4
Make 12

Unit 5
Make 4

Unit 6
Make 1

Unit 7
Make 1

Unit 8
Make 4

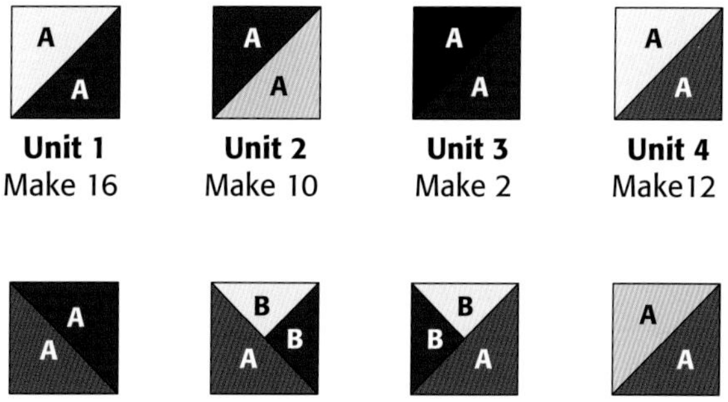

This panda > bear uses the border from *Ruff Patch* on page 4. The bear uses the exact same pieces, just colored differently. Use the graph paper on page 60 to help with your color placement.

Quilting Placement

Referring to the assembly diagram, arrange the patches and units on a design wall. Notice the position of three black patches that represent buttons on the bear's belly. Join the patches and the units to make the sections 1–6. Sew the sections together.

With a tear-away stabilizer on the back, use dark thread and a machine satin stitch about ¼ -wide to embroider the bear's mouth as shown in the quilting placement diagram.

Machine Satin Stitch

Join 12 assorted dark brown D patches with 11 assorted cream D patches as shown to make each of the border #2 side strips. Join 9 assorted dark brown D patches with 8 assorted cream D patches as shown to make each of the border #2 top and bottom strips. Sew a pink E patch to each end as shown.

Matching centers and ends, sew the border #1 side strips to the quilt. Repeat to add the border #1 top and bottom strips. Add border #2 in the same way as border #1.

2 Quilting and Finishing

Beginning in the upper left-hand corner of the background and using the patchwork as a guide, mark a grid over the background as shown. Layer and baste together the backing, batting and quilt top.

In the photographed quilt, brown, pink and cream threads were used for the quilting. Quilt the bear's body and border #1 in the ditch as shown. Quilt the pink accents and eyebrows in the ditch. Quilt circles over the eyes and swirls on the buttons and the feet. Quilt the nose as shown. Quilt the grid. Quilt a looping line in border #1. Meander quilt over the bear's body and border #2 as shown. Bind the quilt. 🐾🐾

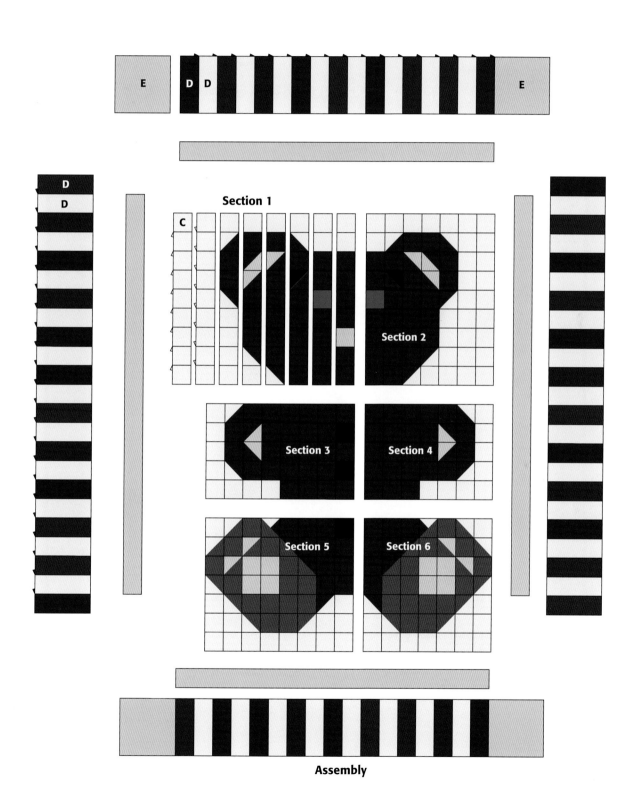

Section 1

Section 2

Section 3

Section 4

Section 5

Section 6

Assembly

Quack Patch

Downy duckling makes a splash

Made by Sheri Ruwe.

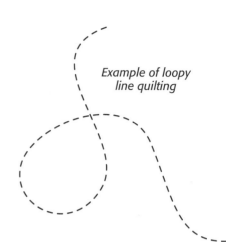

Example of loopy line quilting

materials

Crib: 40¼″ x 50¾″

Assorted Light Blue Tone-on-Tones
⅝ yard *total* for background

Assorted Medium Yellow Tone-on-Tones
⅜ yard *total* for wing and feather on head

Assorted Light Yellow Tone-on-Tones
¾ yard *total* for duck body

Assorted Cheddar Tone-on-Tones
scrap for beak

Assorted Orange Tone-on-Tones
scrap for mouth

Brown Tone-on-Tone
scrap for eyes

Cheddar Tone-on-Tone
⅝ yard for border #1 and cornerstones

Medium Blue Tone-on-Tone
1 yard for border #2 and binding

Light Blue Tone-on-Tone and Light Yellow Tone-on-Tone
⅝ yard *each* for border #2

Backing 2¾ yards (with careful basting, 1 fabric width at 1⅝ yards will be sufficient)

Batting 45″ x 59″

cutting

◹ = cut in half diagonally
⧅ = cut in half twice diagonally

Assorted Light Blue Tone-on-Tones
13 squares 2⅝″ x 2⅝″ ◹ (A)
119 squares (B) 2¼″ x 2¼″

Assorted Medium Yellow Tone-on-Tones
7 squares 2⅝″ x 2⅝″ ◹ (A) (there will be 1 extra)
40 squares (B) 2¼″ x 2¼″

Assorted Light Yellow Tone-on-Tones
20 squares 2⅝″ x 2⅝″ ◹ (A) (there will be 1 extra)
101 squares (B) 2¼″ x 2¼″

Assorted Cheddar Tone-on-Tones
3 squares 2⅝″ x 2⅝″ ◹ (A)
6 squares (B) 2¼″ x 2¼″

Assorted Orange Tone-on-Tones
1 square 2⅝″ x 2⅝″ ◹ (A)
4 squares (B) 2¼″ x 2¼″

Brown Tone-on-Tone
2 squares (B) 2¼″ x 2¼″

Cheddar Tone-on-Tone
for border #1
2 strips 2¼″ x 37¼″ for sides
2 strips 2¼″ x 30¼″ for top/bottom
4 squares (E) 5¾″ x 5¾″

Medium Blue Tone-on-Tone
6 strips 2¼″ x 40″ for binding
10 squares (C) 4¾″ x 4¾″
44 squares (D) 2⅝″ x 2⅝″

Light Blue Tone-on-Tone and Light Yellow Tone-on-Tone
from *each*
10 squares (C) 4¾″ x 4¾″
44 squares (D) 2⅝″ x 2⅝″

1 Making the Quilt Center

Referring to the unit diagrams, pair the A's in the appropriate colors to make the unit 1's–6's as shown.

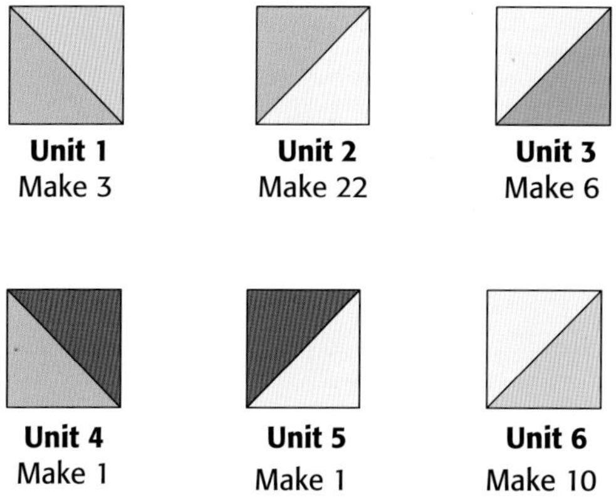

Unit 1
Make 3

Unit 2
Make 22

Unit 3
Make 6

Unit 4
Make 1

Unit 5
Make 1

Unit 6
Make 10

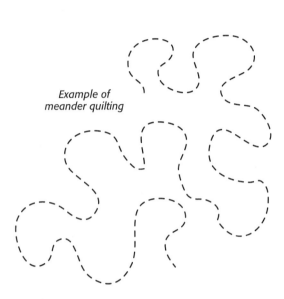

Example of meander quilting

Quilting Placement

Referring to the assembly diagram, join the B's and units to make the sections 1–6. Sew the sections together to make the quilt center.

2 Adding the Borders

To make the border #2 units, refer to the "Fast Flying Geese" technique on page 57. Use the light blue C's and the light yellow D's to make 38 unit 7's (you will have 2 extra). Use the medium blue C's and the light blue D's to make 38 unit 8's (you will have 2 extra). Use the light yellow C's and the medium blue D's to make 38 unit 9's (you will have 2 extra).

Unit 7
Make 38

Unit 8
Make 38

Unit 9
Make 38

Refer to the "Triangle-Squares" technique on page 57 and pair 2 light yellow D's with 2 light blue D's to make 4 unit 10's. Pair 2 light blue D's with 2 medium blue D's to make 4 unit 11's. Pair 2 medium blue D's with 2 yellow D's to make 4 unit 12's.

Unit 10
Make 4

Unit 11
Make 4

Unit 12
Make 4

Refer to the assembly diagram. For each border #2 side strip, join 11 unit 7's–9's and the units 10–12 as shown. For each border #2 top and bottom strip, join 8 unit 7's–9's and units 10–12 as shown; add a cheddar E to each end.

Matching centers and ends, sew the border #1 side strips to the quilt. Repeat to add the border #1 top and bottom strips. Add border #2 in the same way.

3 Quilting and Finishing

Beginning in the upper left-hand corner of the background and using the patchwork as a guide, mark a grid over the background as shown. Layer and baste together the backing, batting and quilt top. Referring to the quilting diagram, quilt the duck's body, wing and beak, border #1 and border #2 in the ditch as shown. Meander quilt over the duck's body. Quilt horizontal lines in the beak and wing. Quilt circles in the eyes. Quilt a looping line in border #1. Quilt 3 overlapping wavy lines in border #2. Bind the quilt. 🐾🐾

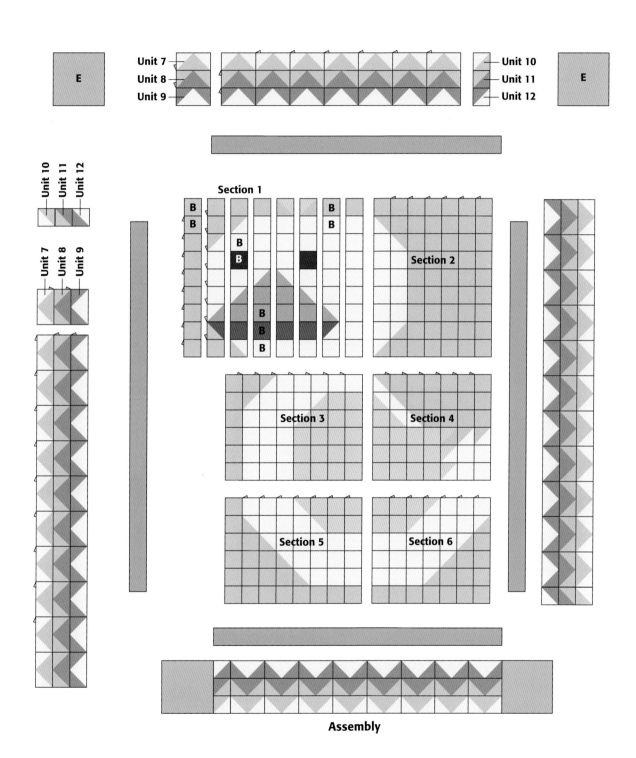

Unit 7
Unit 8
Unit 9

Unit 10
Unit 11
Unit 12

E

E

Unit 10
Unit 11
Unit 12

Unit 7
Unit 8
Unit 9

Section 1

Section 2

Section 3

Section 4

Section 5

Section 6

B

Assembly

Bunny Patch

Hop to it!

Made by Peg Spradlin.

materials

Throw: 40¼" x 50¾"

Assorted Blue Tone-on-Tones
⅝ yard *total* for background

Medium Gray Tone-on-Tone
½ yard for ears and feet

Light Gray Tone-on-Tone #1
⅝ yard for head and arms

Light Pink Tone-on-Tone #1
⅜ yard for ears, nose, feet and border #2

Green Tone-on-Tone
scrap for carrot

Light Gray Tone-on-Tone #2
¼ yard for legs

Orange Tone-on-Tone
¼ yard for carrot

Black Tone-on-Tone
scrap for eyes

White Tone-on-Tone
1 yard for eyes, teeth and border #2

Medium Pink Tone-on-Tone
¾ yard for borders #'s 1 and 2

Dark Pink Tone-on-Tone
¼ yard for border #2

Light Pink Tone-on-Tone #2
½ yard for binding

Backing 2¾ yards (with careful basting, 1 fabric width at 1⅝ yards will be sufficient)

Batting 45" x 59"

Tear-away stabilizer

cutting

☐ = cut in half diagonally
⊠ = cut in half twice diagonally

Assorted Blue Tone-on-Tones
16 squares (A) 2⅝" x 2⅝"
1 square 3" x 3" ⊠ (C) (there will be 2 extra)
77 squares (D) 2¼" x 2¼"

Medium Gray Tone-on-Tone
16 squares (A) 2⅝" x 2⅝"
52 squares (D) 2¼" x 2¼"

Light Gray Tone-on-Tone #1
12 squares (A) 2⅝" x 2⅝"
6 squares 2⅝" x 2⅝" ☐ (B)
3 squares 3" x 3" ⊠ (C)
75 squares (D) 2¼" x 2¼"

Light Pink Tone-on-Tone #1
2 strips 2¼" x 40" for band A's
3 squares (A) 2⅝" x 2⅝"
1 square 3" x 3" ⊠ (C)
11 squares (D) 2¼" x 2¼"

Green Tone-on-Tone
2 squares (A) 2⅝" x 2⅝"
2 squares (D) 2¼" x 2¼"

Light Gray Tone-on-Tone #2
6 squares (A) 2⅝" x 2⅝"
1 square 2⅝" x 2⅝" ☐ (B) (there will be 1 extra)
1 square 3" x 3" ⊠ (C) (there will be 3 extra)
12 squares (D) 2¼" x 2¼"

Orange Tone-on-Tone
3 squares (A) 2⅝" x 2⅝"
1 square 3" x 3" ⊠ (C) (there will be 1 extra)
13 squares (D) 2¼" x 2¼"

Black Tone-on-Tone
1 square 3" x 3" ⊠ (C)

White Tone-on-Tone
4 strips 4" x 40" for band A's and C's
4 strips 2¼" x 40" for band B's
1 square 2⅝" x 2⅝" ☐ (B)
1 square 3" x 3" ⊠ (C)
1 square (D) 2¼" x 2¼"

Medium Pink Tone-on-Tone
for border #1
2 strips 2¼" x 37¼" for sides
2 strips 2¼" x 30¼" for top/bottom
2 strips 2¼" x 40" for band B's
4 squares (E) 5¾" x 5¾"

Dark Pink Tone-on-Tone
2 strips 2¼" x 40" for band C's

Light Pink Tone-on-Tone #2
6 strips 2¼" x 40" for binding

1 About This Quilt
We used 3 grays in the bunny: a medium gray for the ears and feet, light gray #1 for the head and arms and light gray #2 for the legs.

2 Making the Quilt Center
Refer to the "Triangle-Squares" technique on page 57 and the chart at right for the appropriate grays; pair A's in the colors shown in the diagrams to make the unit 1's–10's.

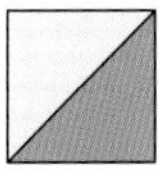

	medium gray A's	light gray #1 A's	light gray #2 A's
unit 1	10		
unit 2		6	
unit 3		1	
unit 4	1	1	
unit 5		2	
unit 6		1	1
unit 7		1	
unit 8			2
unit 9	2		
unit 10	3		3

    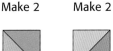 

Unit 1 Make 20
Unit 2 Make 11
Unit 3 Make 2
Unit 4 Make 2
Unit 5 Make 4

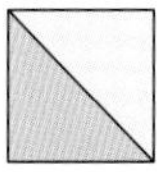

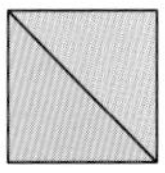

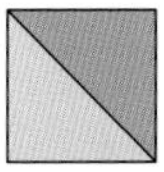

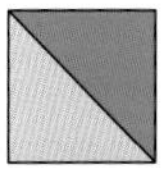

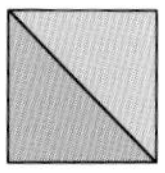

Unit 6 Make 2
Unit 7 Make 2
Unit 8 Make 4
Unit 9 Make 4
Unit 10 Make 6

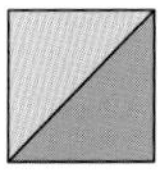

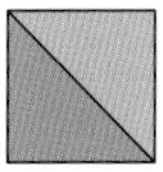

To make a unit 11, join a white C and black C; join to a white B as shown to complete the unit. In the same way, make unit 12's–16's using the light gray #1 B's and C's. Make 1 unit 17 using the light gray #2 B and C.

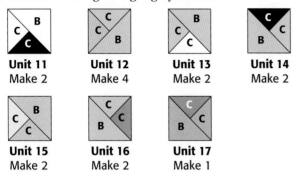

| Unit 11
Make 2 | Unit 12
Make 4 | Unit 13
Make 2 | Unit 14
Make 2 |

| Unit 15
Make 2 | Unit 16
Make 2 | Unit 17
Make 1 |

Refer to the assembly diagram; join D's and units as shown to make the sections 1–6. Sew the sections together to make the quilt center.

With a tear-away stabilizer on the back, use dark thread and a machine satin stitch about ¼"-wide to embroider the bunny's mouth as shown in the quilting placement diagram.

Machine Satin Stitch

Quilting Placement

3 Adding the Borders

Matching centers and ends, sew the border #1 side strips to the quilt. Repeat to add the border #1 top and bottom strips.

Refer to the diagrams to make the border #2 units. Sew a light pink strip and a 4" white strip together to make each of the 2 band A's.

Join a 2¼" medium pink strip with 2¼" white strips as shown to make each of the 2 band B's.

Join a dark pink strip and a 4" white strip to make each of the 2 band C's.

Cut each band in 2¼" increments to make 24 unit 18's from the band A's, 28 unit 19's from the band B's and 28 unit 20's from the band C's.

Refer to the assembly diagram. For each border #2 side strip, join 7 unit 18's, 8 unit 19's and 8 unit 20's as shown. For each border #2 top and bottom strip, join 5 unit 18's, 6 unit 19's and 6 unit 20's as shown; add an E to each end.

Add border #2 to the quilt in the same way as border #1.

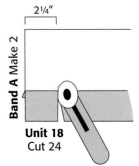

Band A Make 2

2¼"

Unit 18
Cut 24

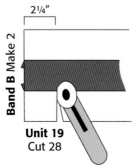

Band B Make 2

2¼"

Unit 19
Cut 28

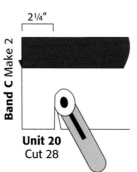

Band C Make 2

2¼"

Unit 20
Cut 28

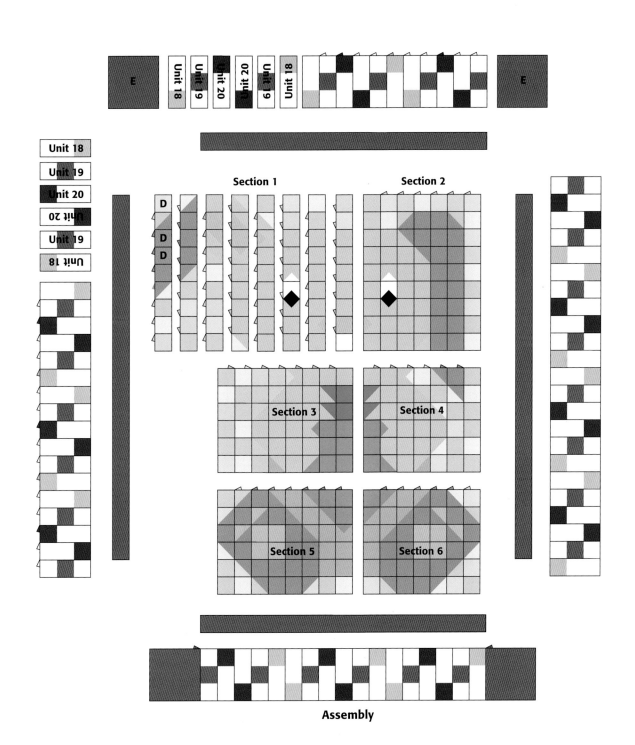

Assembly

4 Quilting and Finishing

Refer to the quilting diagram; beginning in the upper left-hand corner of the background and using the patchwork as a guide, mark a grid over the background as shown. Layer and baste together the backing, batting and quilt top.

Quilt the bunny's body, ears, arms, feet, carrot and border #1 in the ditch as shown. Quilt straight lines on the ears, feet and carrot as shown. Quilt details to the carrot top, nose and bottom of the feet as shown. Meander quilt on the bunny and in border #2. Quilt the marked grid. Quilt a looping line in border #1. Bind the quilt. 🐾🐾

Banana Patch

Play with a whimsical monkey

Made by Peg Spradlin.

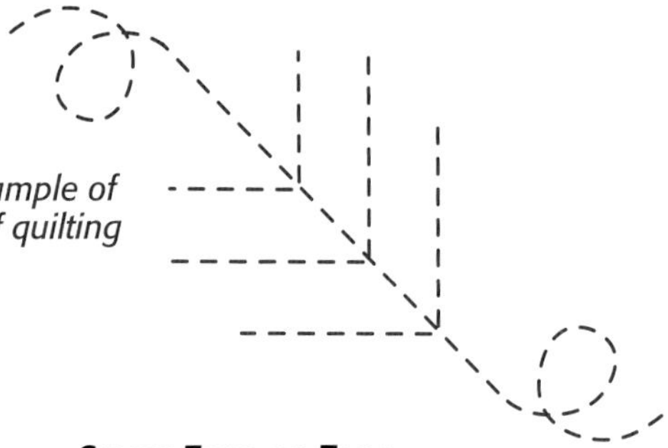

Example of leaf quilting

materials

Crib: 40¼" x 50¾"

Assorted Medium Green Tone-on-Tones
1⅜ yards *total* for background and border #2

Assorted Dark Brown Tone-on-Tones
½ yard *total* for monkey

Medium Brown Tone-on-Tone
½ yard for monkey

Yellow Tone-on-Tone
scraps for banana

Cream Tone-on-Tone
⅜ yard for monkey

White Tone-on-Tone
scraps for eyes

Black Tone-on-Tone
scraps for eyes and nose

Medium Blue Tone-on-Tone
1 yard for border #1, border #2 and binding

Light Blue Tone-on-Tone
1 yard for border #2

Backing 2¾ yards (with careful basting, 1 fabric width at 1⅝ yards will be sufficient)

Batting 45" x 59"

Tear-away stabilizer

cutting

 = cut in half diagonally
⊠ = cut in half twice diagonally

Assorted Medium Green Tone-on-Tones
23 squares (A) 2⅝" x 2⅝"
1 square 3" x 3" ⊠ (C) (there will be 2 extra)
139 squares (D) 2¼" x 2¼"
24 squares (E) 4" x 4"

Assorted Dark Brown Tone-on-Tones
19 squares (A) 2⅝" x 2⅝"
2 squares 2⅝" x 2⅝" ◩ (B)
2 squares 3" x 3" ⊠ (C) (there will be 3 extra)
46 squares (D) 2¼" x 2¼"

Medium Brown Tone-on-Tone
3 squares (A) 2⅝" x 2⅝"
2 squares 2⅝" x 2⅝" ◩ (B) (there will be 1 extra)
1 square 3" x 3" ⊠ (C) (there will be 1 extra)
34 squares (D) 2¼" x 2¼"

Yellow Tone-on-Tone
3 squares (A) 2⅝" x 2⅝"
3 squares (D) 2¼" x 2¼"

Cream Tone-on-Tone
6 squares (A) 2⅝" x 2⅝"
1 square 2⅝" x 2⅝" ◩ (B) (there will be 1 extra)
1 square 3" x 3" ⊠ (C) (there will be 1 extra)
29 squares (D) 2¼" x 2¼"

White Tone-on-Tone
1 square 2⅝" x 2⅝" ◩ (B)
1 square 3" x 3" ⊠ (C)

Black Tone-on-Tone
1 square 3" x 3" ⊠ (C) (there will be 1 extra)

Medium Blue Tone-on-Tone
for border #1
2 strips 2¼" x 37¼" for sides
2 strips 2¼" x 30¼" for top/bottom
6 strips 2¼" x 40" for binding
4 squares (J) 5¾" x 5¾"

Light Blue Tone-on-Tone
48 squares (F) 1⅞" x 1⅞"
48 rectangles (G) 1⅜" x 4"
48 rectangles (H) 1⅜" x 5¾"
8 rectangles (I) 2¼" x 5¾"

---

1 Making the Quilt Center

Refer to the "Triangle-Squares" technique on page 57; pair A's in the colors shown in the diagrams to make the unit 1's–5's.

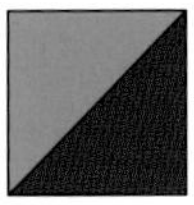

To make a unit 6, join a cream C and dark brown C; join to a dark brown B as shown to complete the unit. Make 2 unit 6's. In the same way, make unit 7–11's.

Unit 1
Make 32

Unit 2
Make 6

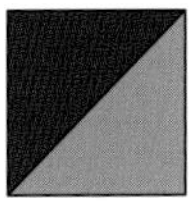

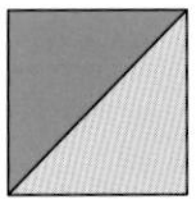

Unit 3
Make 4

Unit 4
Make 10

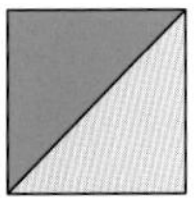

Unit 5
Make 2

Unit 6
Make 2

Unit 7
Make 1

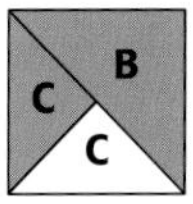

Unit 8
Make 2

Unit 9
Make 2

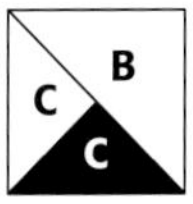

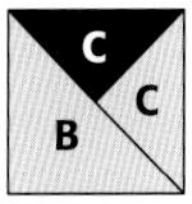

Unit 10
Make 1

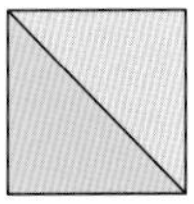

Unit 11
Make 2

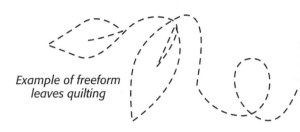

Example of freeform leaves quilting

Refer to the assembly diagram; join D's and units as shown to make sections 1–6. Sew the sections together to make the quilt center.

With a tear-away stabilizer on the back, use dark thread and a machine satin stitch about ¼"-wide to embroider the monkey's mouth as shown in the quilting placement diagram.

Machine Satin Stitch

2 Adding the Borders

Matching centers and ends, sew the border #1 side strips to the quilt. Repeat to add the border #1 top and bottom strips.

Refer to the "Stitch-and-Flip" technique on page 57. Use a green E and 2 light blue F's to make a unit 12 as shown. Make 24 unit 12's.

Join G's and H's to a unit 12 as shown to make a block. Make 24 blocks.

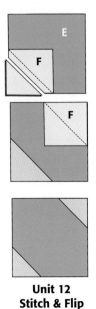

Unit 12
Stitch & Flip
Make 24

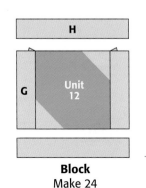

Block
Make 24

Quilting Placement

Refer to the assembly diagram. For each border #2 side strip, join 7 blocks as shown; add an I to each end. For each border #2 top and bottom strip, join 5 blocks as shown; add an I and a medium blue J to each end. Add border #2 in the same way as border #1.

3 Quilting and Finishing

Refer to the quilting diagram; beginning in the upper left-hand corner of the background and using the patchwork as a guide, mark a grid over the background as shown. Layer and baste together the backing, batting and quilt top.

Quilt the monkey, banana and border #1 in the ditch as shown. Quilt straight lines on the banana as shown. Quilt ovals around the eyes and nose as shown. Meander quilt on the monkey. Quilt the marked grid. Quilt a looping line in border #1. Quilt lines to resemble veins in a leaf in the border #2 blocks, connecting the leaves with a loopy line and leaves in the corners as shown. Bind the quilt. 🐾🐾

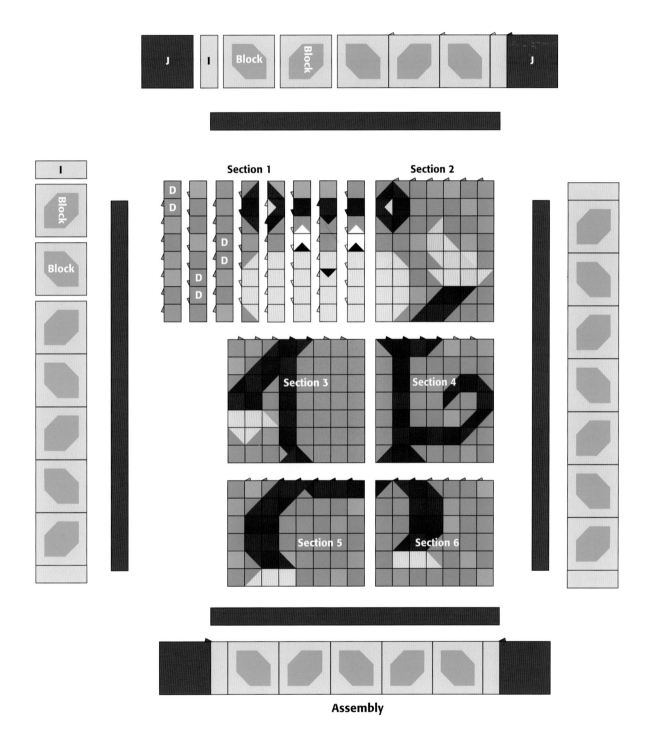

Assembly

Prickly Patch

Curl up with an adorable hedgehog

Made by Peg Spradlin.

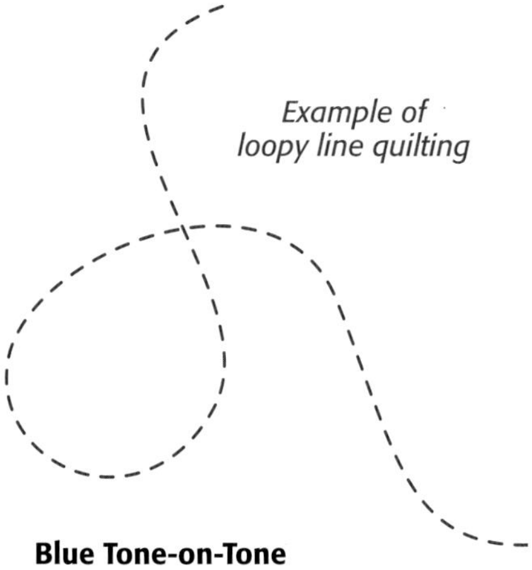

materials

Crib: 42¼" x 50¾"

Assorted Green Tone-on-Tones
⅝ yard *total* for background
Assorted Brown Tone-on-Tones
¾ yard *total* for hedgehog
Black and Pink Tone-on-Tones
scraps for nose and mouth
Tan Tone-on-Tone
scraps for feet
White Tone-on-Tone
scraps for eye
Assorted Cream Tone-on-Tones
⅝ yard *total* for hedgehog
Blue Tone-on-Tone
1 yard for eye, border #1, cornerstones and binding
Light Brown Tone-on-Tone
½ yard for border #2
Medium Brown Tone-on-Tone
⅝ yard for border #2
Dark Brown Tone-on-Tone
⅜ yard for border #2
Backing 2¾ yards (with careful basting, 1 fabric width at 1⅝ yards will be
sufficient)
Batting 45" x 59"

cutting

☐ = cut in half diagonally
☒ = cut in half twice diagonally

Assorted Green Tone-on-Tones
17 squares 2⅝" x 2⅝" ☐ (A) (there
will be 1 extra)
81 squares (D) 2¼" x 2¼"
Assorted Brown Tone-on-Tones
22 squares 2⅝" x 2⅝" ☐ (A) (there
will be 1 extra)
104 squares (D) 2¼" x 2¼"
Black and Pink Tone-on-Tones
from *each*
1 square 2⅝" x 2⅝" ☐ (A) (there
will be 1 extra from each)
Tan Tone-on-Tone
2 squares 2⅝" x 2⅝" ☐ (A)
3 squares (D) 2¼" x 2¼"
White Tone-on-Tone
1 square 2⅝" x 2⅝" ☐ (A) (there
will be 1 extra)
1 square 3" x 3" ☒ (B) (there will
be 2 extra)
Assorted Cream Tone-on-Tones
13 squares 2⅝" x 2⅝" ☐ (A)
1 square 3" x 3" ☒ (B) (there will
be 2 extra)
71 squares (D) 2¼" x 2¼"

Blue Tone-on-Tone
for border #1
2 strips 2¼" x 37¼" for sides
2 strips 2¼" x 30¼" for top/bottom
6 strips 2¼" x 40" for binding
1 square 3" x 3" ☒ (B) (there will
be 2 extra)
4 squares (E) 5¾" x 5¾"
Light Brown Tone-on-Tone
80 squares (C) 2⅝" x 2⅝"
Medium Brown Tone-on-Tone
80 squares (C) 2⅝" x 2⅝"
Dark Brown Tone-on-Tone
for border #2
2 strips 2¼" x 40¾" for sides
2 strips 2¼" x 30¼" for top/bottom

Example of loopy line quilting

1 About This Quilt

Notice that assorted creams are used for the hedgehog's body, tan for the feet and light brown in border #2.

2 Making the Quilt Center

Pairing the A's in the appropriate colors, and noting that the tan A's are used in units 6–8, make the unit 1's–8's as shown.

Unit 1
Make 26

Unit 2
Make 1

Unit 3
Make 5

Unit 4
Make 16

Unit 5
Make 1

Unit 6
Make 1

Unit 7
Make 2

Unit 8
Make 1

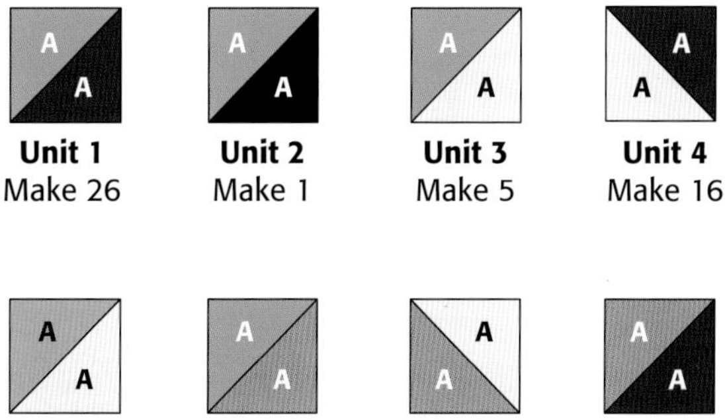

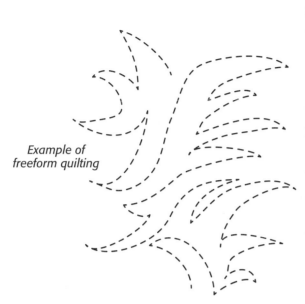

Example of freeform quilting

Quilting Placement

To make a unit 9, join a cream B and white B; join to a cream A as shown to complete the unit 9. In the same way, join a white B and blue B to a white A to make a unit 10; join a cream B and blue B to a cream A to make a unit 11.

Unit 9
Make 1

Unit 10
Make 1

Unit 11
Make 1

Referring to the assembly diagram, join the D's and units to make the sections 1–6. Sew the sections together to make the quilt center.

3 Adding the Borders

Matching centers and ends, sew the border #1 side strips to the quilt. Add the border #1 top and bottom strips in the same way.

Refer to the "Triangle-Squares" technique on page 57. Pair each light brown C with a medium brown C to make 160 unit 12's.

**Unit 12
from C's**
Make 160

Refer to the assembly diagram. Noting the orientations, sew 4 sets of 23 unit 12's together as shown for the border #2 sides; join to the dark brown border #2 side strips as shown.

In the same way, sew 4 sets of 17 unit 12's together as shown for the border #2 top/bottom; join to the dark brown border #2 top and bottom strips as shown. Sew a blue E to each end of the border #2 top and bottom strips.

Add border #2 to the quilt top in the same way as border #1.

4 Quilting and Finishing

Beginning in the upper left-hand corner of the background and using the patchwork as a guide, mark a grid over the background as shown. Layer and baste together the backing, batting and quilt top.

Quilt the hedgehog, nose, mouth, feet, border #1 and border #2 in the ditch as shown. Quilt the border #2 design into the cornerstones (E) as shown. Quilt circles over the eyes. Quilt curved lines on the hedgehog's back. Meander quilt on the cream areas of the hedgehog's body. Quilt details on the feet as shown. Quilt the marked grid. Quilt a looping line in border #1.

Bind the quilt. 🐾🐾

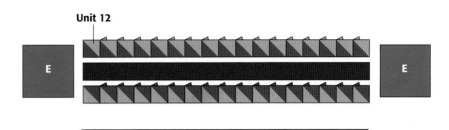

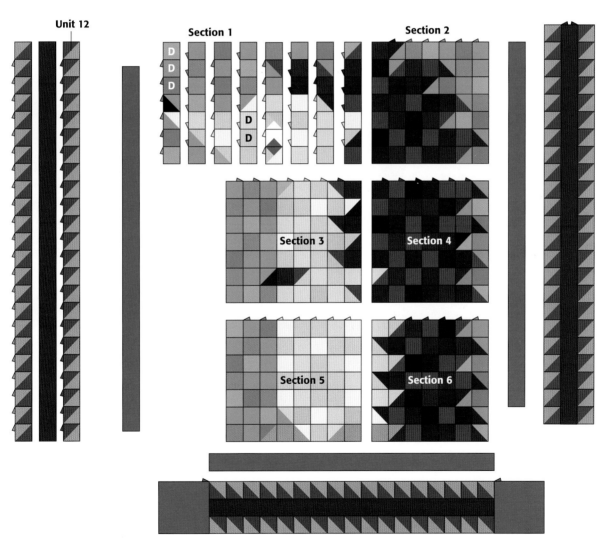

Assembly

Peanut Patch

Small quilt displays a jumbo friend

Made by Peg Spradlin.

materials

Crib: 40¼" x 50¾"

Assorted Light Blue Tone-on-Tones
¾ yard *total* for background
Medium Gray Tone-on-Tone
¾ yard for elephant
Dark Gray Tone-on-Tone
⅜ yard for ears and feet
Medium Blue Tone-on-Tone
⅞ yard for eye and border #2
Yellow Tone-on-Tone
⅝ yard for stars
White Tone-on-Tone
scraps for tusk
Green Tone-on-Tone
⅛ yard for pedestal
Purple Tone-on-Tone
1 yard for pedestal, border #'s 1and 2
and binding
Backing 2¾ yards (with careful basting, 1 fabric width at 1⅝ yards will be
sufficient)
Batting 45" x 59"

cutting

◰ = cut in half diagonally
⊠ = cut in half twice diagonally

Assorted Light Blue Tone-on-Tones
12 squares 2⅝" x 2⅝" ◰ (A) (there
will be 1 extra)
1 square 3" x 3" ⊠ (B) (there will be
3 extra)
112 squares (C) 2¼" x 2¼"
Medium Gray Tone-on-Tone
17 squares 2⅝" x 2⅝" ◰ (A)
1 square 3" x 3" ⊠ (B) (there will be
3 extra)
116 squares (C) 2¼" x 2¼"
Dark Gray Tone-on-Tone
7 squares 2⅝" x 2⅝" ◰ (A)
31 squares (C) 2¼" x 2¼"
Medium Blue Tone-on-Tone
1 square 2⅝" x 2⅝" ◰ (A) (there
will be 1 extra)
96 squares (C) 2¼" x 2¼"
48 squares (D) 2⅝" x 2⅝"
8 rectangles (E) 2¼" x 5¾"
Yellow Tone-on-Tone
24 squares (C) 2¼" x 2¼"
48 squares (D) 2⅝" x 2⅝"

White Tone-on-Tone
2 squares 2⅝" x 2⅝" ◰ (A) (there
will be 1 extra)
3 squares (C) 2¼" x 2¼"
Green Tone-on-Tone
10 squares (C) 2¼" x 2¼"
Purple Tone-on-Tone
for border #1
2 strips 2¼" x 37¼" for sides
2 strips 2¼" x 30¼" for top/bottom
6 strips 2¼" x 40" for binding
5 squares (C) 2¼" x 2¼"
4 squares (F) 5¾" x 5¾"

1 Making the Quilt Center

Pairing the A's in the appropriate colors, make the
unit 1's–6 as shown.

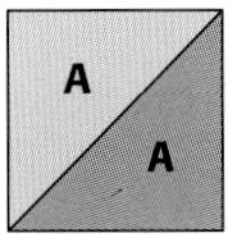

To make a unit 7, join a light blue B and medium gray B;
join to a medium gray A as shown to complete the unit.

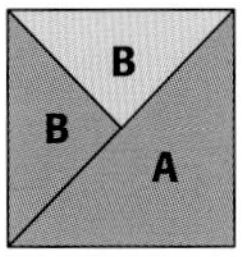

Unit 1
Make 19

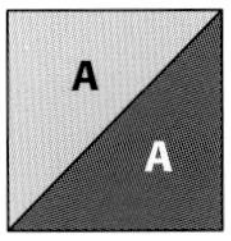

Unit 2
Make 3

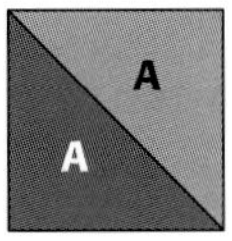

Unit 3
Make 11

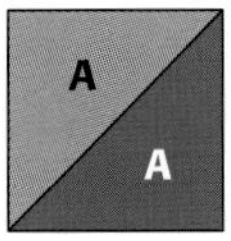

Unit 7
Make 1

Unit 4
Make 1

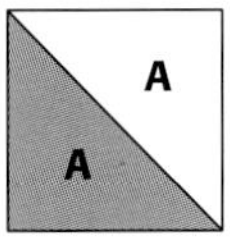

Unit 5
Make 2

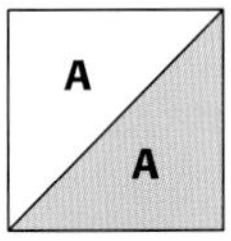

Unit 6
Make 1

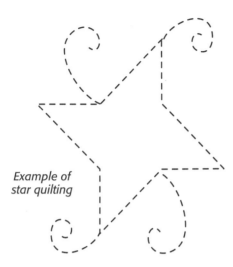

Example of star quilting

Refer to the assembly diagram; join the C's and units as shown to make the sections 1–6. Sew the sections together to make the quilt center.

2 Adding the Borders

Matching centers and ends, sew the border #1 side strips to the quilt. Add the border #1 top and bottom strips in the same way.

Refer to the "Triangle-Squares" technique on page 57. Pair each medium blue D with a yellow D to make 96 unit 8's.

Unit 8
Make 96

The only difference between block Y's and block Z's is the orientation of the unit 8's. Join medium blue C's, yellow C's and unit 8's as shown to make 14 block Y's and 10 block Z's.

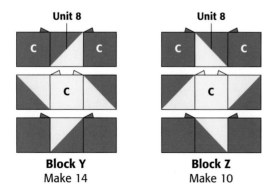

Block Y
Make 14

Block Z
Make 10

Refer to the assembly diagram. Join 4 block Y's, 3 block Z's and 2 E's as shown to make each of the border #2 side strips.

Quilting Placement

Join 3 block Y's, 2 block Z's and 2 E's as shown to make the border #2 top and bottom strips; sew a purple F to each end.

Add border #2 to the quilt top in the same way as border #1.

3 Quilting and Finishing

Beginning in the upper left-hand corner of the background and using the patchwork as a guide, mark a grid over the background as shown. Layer and baste together the backing, batting and quilt top.

Quilt the elephant, ear, tusk, feet, pedestal and border #1 in the ditch as shown. Quilt a circle around the eye as shown. Echo quilt within the ear. Meander quilt on the head, trunk and body. Quilt the marked grid. Quilt a looping line in border #1. Quilt the border #2 stars in the ditch, adding curls as shown and similar stars in the cornerstones.

Bind the quilt. 🐾🐾

Assembly

Hoo Patch

Welcome the night with a wise old friend

Made by Peg Spradlin.

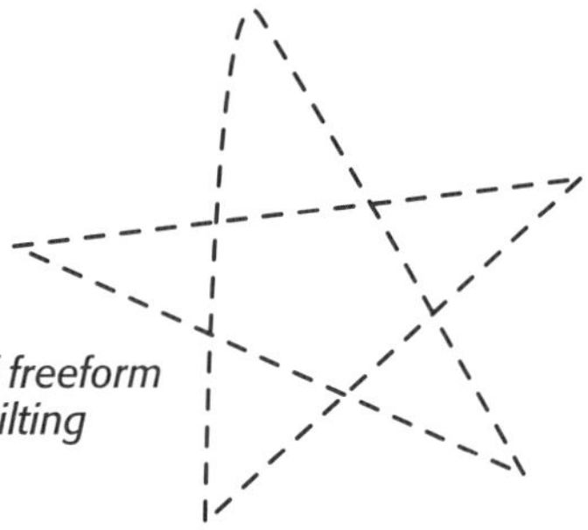

Example of freeform star quilting

materials

Crib: 40¼" x 50¾"

Medium Blue Tone-on-Tone
⅜ yard for background

Dark Brown Tone-on-Tone
⅝ yard for owl

Medium Brown Tone-on-Tone
⅝ yard for owl

Light Brown Tone-on-Tone
⅜ yard for owl

White Tone-on-Tone
fat eighth for eyes (a fat eighth is approximately 9" x 20")

Orange Tone-on-Tone
fat eighth for beak and talons

Black Tone-on-Tone
fat quarter for eyes and branch (a fat quarter is approximately 18" x 20")

Light Blue Tone-on-Tone
⅞ yard for border #2

Light Gray Tone-on-Tone
⅜ yard for border #2

Dark Blue Tone-on-Tone
1 yard for border #'s 1 and 2 and binding

Backing 2¾ yards (with careful basting, 1 fabric width at 1⅝ yards will be sufficient)

Batting 45" x 59"

cutting

▱ = cut in half diagonally

⊠ = cut in half twice diagonally

Medium Blue Tone-on-Tone
6 squares (A) 2⅝" x 2⅝"
53 squares (D) 2¼" x 2¼"

Dark Brown Tone-on-Tone
9 squares (A) 2⅝" x 2⅝"
2 squares 3" x 3" ⊠ (C)
68 squares (D) 2¼" x 2¼"

Medium Brown Tone-on-Tone
9 squares (A) 2⅝" x 2⅝"
5 squares 2⅝" x 2⅝" ▱ (B) (there will be 1 extra)
3 squares 3" x 3" ⊠ (C) (there will be 2 extra)
80 squares (D) 2¼" x 2¼"

Light Brown Tone-on-Tone
8 squares (A) 2⅝" x 2⅝"
1 square 2⅝" x 2⅝" ▱ (B) (there will be 1 extra)
1 square 3" x 3" ⊠ (C) (there will be 3 extra)
24 squares (D) 2¼" x 2¼"

White Tone-on-Tone
4 squares (A) 2⅝" x 2⅝"
8 squares (D) 2¼" x 2¼"

Orange Tone-on-Tone
2 squares (A) 2⅝" x 2⅝"
2 squares 3" x 3" ⊠ (C) (there will be 1 extra)
8 squares (D) 2¼" x 2¼"

Black Tone-on-Tone
3 squares 2⅝" x 2⅝" ▱ (B)
2 squares 3" x 3" ⊠ (C) (there will be 2 extra)
20 squares (D) 2¼" x 2¼"

Light Blue Tone-on-Tone
24 squares (A) 2⅝" x 2⅝"
36 squares (D) 2¼" x 2¼"
8 squares (E) 5¾" x 5¾"
4 rectangles (F) 5¾" x 7½"
4 rectangles (G) 2¼" x 5¾"

Light Gray Tone-on-Tone
24 squares (A) 2⅝" x 2⅝"
24 squares (D) 2¼" x 2¼"

Dark Blue Tone-on-Tone
for border #1
2 strips 2¼" x 37¼" for sides
2 strips 2¼" x 30¼" for top/bottom
6 strips 2¼" x 40" for binding
4 squares (E) 5¾" x 5¾"

1 Making the Quilt Center

Refer to the "Triangle-Squares" technique on page 57; pair A's in the colors shown in the diagrams to make the unit 1's–7's.

To make a unit 8, join a light brown C and medium brown C; join to a medium brown B as shown to complete the unit. In the same way, make unit 9–11's in the colors shown.

Unit 1
Make 10

Unit 2
Make 2

Unit 3
Make 8

Unit 4
Make 6

Unit 8
Make 1

Unit 9
Make 1

Unit 10
Make 8

Unit 11
Make 6

Unit 5
Make 8

Unit 6
Make 2

Unit 7
Make 2

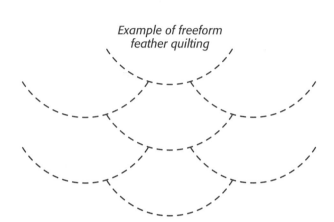

*Example of freeform
feather quilting*

Refer to the assembly diagram; join the D's and units as shown to make sections 1–6. Sew the sections together to make the quilt center.

2 Adding the Borders

Matching centers and ends, sew the border #1 side strips to the quilt. Repeat to add the border #1 top and bottom strips.

Using the triangle-squares technique, pair light blue tone-on-tone A's with light gray A's to make 48 unit 12's.

Unit 12
Make 48

Join unit 12's, light blue D's and light gray D's as shown to make a block. Make 12 blocks.

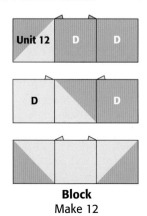

Block
Make 12

Quilting Placement

Refer to the assembly diagram. For each border #2 side strip, join 3 blocks, 2 light blue E's and 2 light blue F's as shown. For each border #2 top and bottom strip, join 3 blocks, 2 light blue E's and 2 light blue G's as shown; add a dark blue E to each end. Add border #2 in the same way as border #1.

3 Quilting and Finishing

Refer to the quilting diagram; beginning in the upper left-hand corner of the background and using the patchwork as a guide, mark a grid over the background as shown. Layer and baste together the backing, batting and quilt top.

Quilt the owl, branch, border #1 and the moons in border #2 in the ditch as shown. Quilt the marked grid.

Quilt straight lines on the wings and ears and curves on the chest as shown. Meander quilt on the face. Quilt gentle waves on the branch. Quilt a looping line in border #1. Quilt stars in border #2, connecting the stars with a loopy line as shown.

Bind the quilt. 🐾🐾

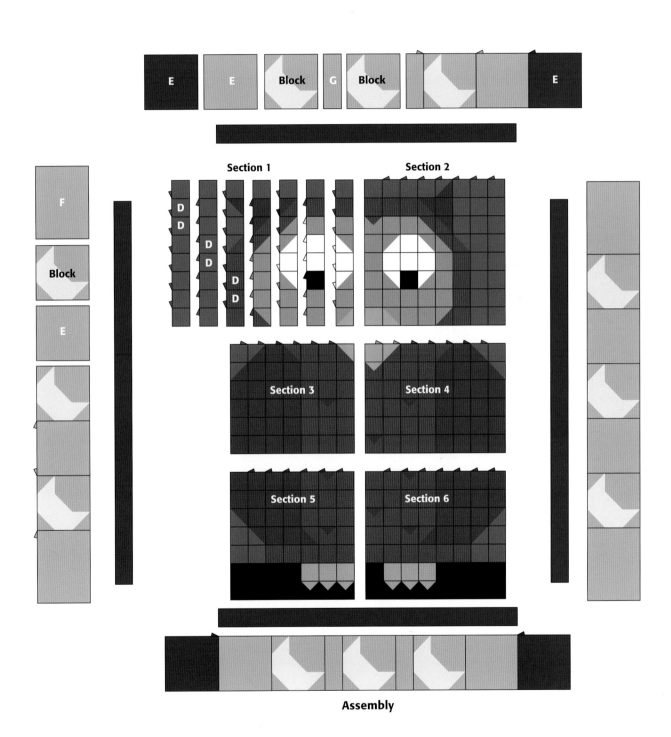

quiltmaker.com (39)

Pokey Patch

No time for slow and steady? This quilt is quickly ready

Made by Peg Spradlin.

materials

Crib: 40¼" x 50¾"

Assorted Cream Tone-on-Tones
¾ yard *total* for background
Assorted Green Tone-on-Tones
⅝ yard *total* for turtle
Assorted Black Tone-on-Tones
¼ yard *total* for eyes and shell
Brown Tone-on-Tone #1
⅛ yard for shell
Brown Tone-on-Tone #2
¼ yard for shell
Brown Tone-on-Tone #3
¼ yard for shell
Brown Tone-on-Tone #4
¼ yard for shell
Medium Blue Tone-on-Tone
⅝ yard for border #2
Green Tone-on-Tone
1⅛ yards for border #1, border #2
and binding
Light Blue Tone-on-Tone
⅜ yard for border #2
Black Tone-on-Tone
½ yard for border #2
Backing 2¾ yards (with careful basting, 1 fabric width at 1⅝ yards will be
sufficient)
Batting 45" x 55"

cutting

◩ = cut in half diagonally
◪ = cut in half twice diagonally

Assorted Cream Tone-on-Tones
17 squares 2⅝" x 2⅝" ◩ (A)
(there will be 1 extra)
1 square 3" x 3" ◪ (B) (there will
be 3 extra)
109 squares (C) 2¼" x 2¼"
Assorted Green Tone-on-Tones
19 squares 2⅝" x 2⅝" ◩ (A)
1 square 3" x 3" ◪ (B) (there will
be 3 extra)
55 squares (C) 2¼" x 2¼"
Assorted Black Tone-on-Tones
25 squares 2⅝" x 2⅝" ◩ (A)
■ **Brown Tone-on-Tone #1**
6 squares 2⅝" x 2⅝" cut diagonally
to yield 12 triangles ◩ (A)
8 squares (C) 2¼" x 2¼"
■ **Brown Tone-on-Tone #2**
9 squares 2⅝" x 2⅝" ◩ (A) (there
will be 1 extra)
17 squares (C) 2¼" x 2¼"

■ **Brown Tone-on-Tone #3**
9 squares 2⅝" x 2⅝" ◩ (A)
(there will be 1 extra)
17 squares (C) 2¼" x 2¼"
■ **Brown Tone-on-Tone #4**
7 squares 2⅝" x 2⅝" ◩ (A)
18 squares (C) 2¼" x 2¼"
Medium Blue Tone-on-Tone
4 strips 2¼" x 40" for bands
28 rectangles (F) 2¼" x 4"
Green Tone-on-Tone
2 strips 2¼" x 40" for bands
for border #1
2 strips 2¼" x 37¼" for sides
2 strips 2¼" x 30¼" for top/bottom
6 strips 2¼" x 40" for binding
4 squares (G) 5¾" x 5¾"
Light Blue Tone-on-Tone
14 squares (D) 4¾" x 4¾"
Black Tone-on-Tone
56 squares (E) 2⅝" x 2⅝"

1 Making the Quilt Center

Pair the A's in the appropriate colors to make the unit 1's
and 2's as shown. To make the unit 3, join a cream B and a
green B; join to a cream A as shown to complete the unit.

Unit 1
Make 28

Unit 2
Make 2

Unit 3
Make 1

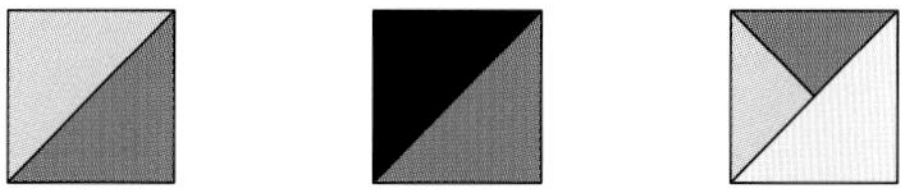

Notice the arrangement of the brown tone-on-tones on
the turtle's shell. Refer to the chart at right to pair the
green, black or cream A's with the appropriate brown
tone-on-tone A's to make unit 4's–6's as shown.

Unit 4
Make 8

Unit 5
Make 48

Unit 6
Make 4

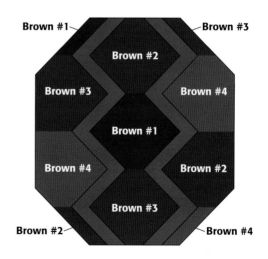

	unit 4	unit 5	unit 6
brown #1	2	10	0
brown #2	2	14	1
brown #3	2	14	1
brown #4	2	10	2

Example of continuous circle quilting

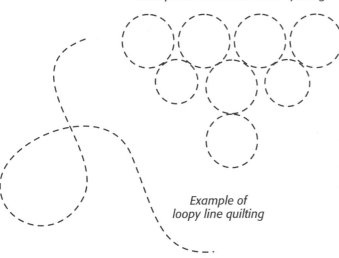

Example of loopy line quilting

Referring to the assembly diagram, join the C's and units to make the sections 1–6. Sew the sections together to make the quilt center.

2 Adding the Borders

To make the border #2 units, join a green strip with 2 medium blue strips as shown to make a band. Make 2 bands. Cut each band in 2¼" increments to make 24 unit 7's. Refer to the "Fast Flying Geese" technique on page 57. Using the light blue D's and black E's, make 56 unit 8's.

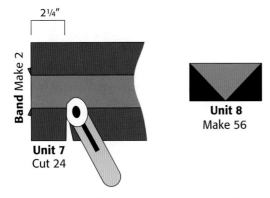

2¼"

Band Make 2

Unit 7
Cut 24

Unit 8
Make 56

Refer to the assembly diagram. For each border #2 side strip, join 8 F's, 16 unit 8's and 7 unit 7's as shown. For each border #2 top and bottom strip, join 6 F's, 12 unit 8's and 5 unit 7's as shown; add a green G to each end.

Matching centers and ends, sew the border #1 side strips to the quilt. Repeat to add the border #1 top and bottom strips. Add border #2 in the same way.

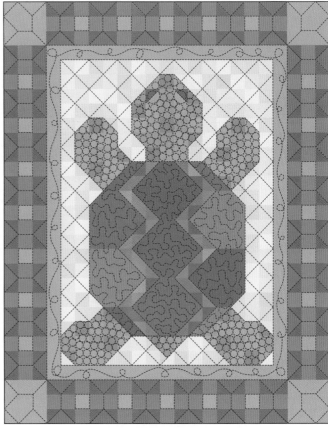

Quilting Placement

3 Quilting and Finishing

Beginning in the upper left-hand corner of the background and using the patchwork as a guide, mark a grid over the background as shown. Layer and baste together the backing, batting and quilt top.

Referring to the quilting diagram, quilt the turtle, shell, border #1 and border #2 in the ditch as shown. Meander quilt over the turtle's shell. Quilt circles around each eye and small continuous circles on the head, legs and tail as shown. Quilt the marked grid. Quilt a looping line in border #1. Quilt lines in the G's as shown. Bind the quilt. 🐾🐾

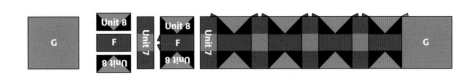

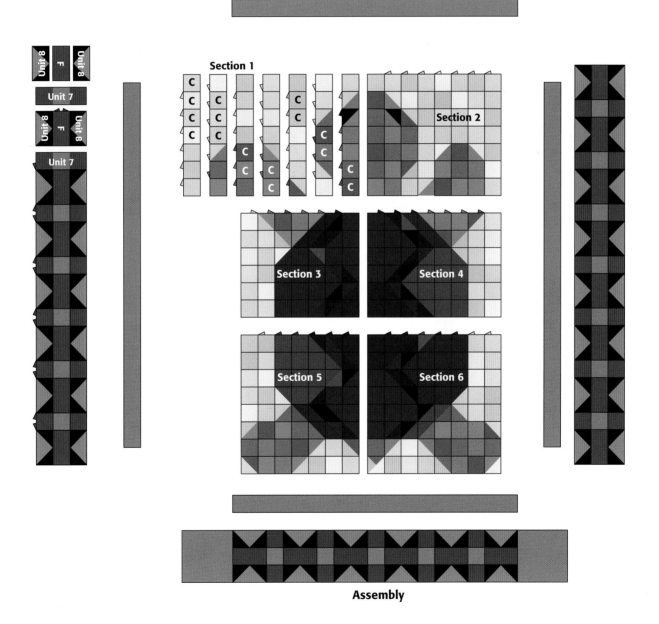

Assembly

Polar Patch

Keeping a little pal cozy and warm

Made by Peg Spradlin.

materials

Crib: 40¼" x 50¾"

Assorted Blue Tone-on-Tones
⅝ yard *total* for background

Assorted Black Tone-on-Tones
½ yard *total* for penguins

Assorted White Tone-on-Tones
¾ yard *total* for penguins

Light Gray Tone-on-Tone
⅛ yard for small penguin

Yellow Tone-on-Tone
1 yard for penguin, border #'s 1 and 2
and binding

Medium Gray Tone-on-Tone
scrap for small penguin

Light Blue Tone-on-Tone
¾ yard for border #2

White Tone-on-Tone
⅝ yard for border #2

Medium Blue Tone-on-Tone
½ yard for border #2

Backing 2¾ yards (with careful basting, 1 fabric width at 1⅝ yards will be
sufficient)

Batting 45" x 59"

cutting

▢ = cut in half diagonally
⊠ = cut in half twice diagonally

Assorted Blue Tone-on-Tones
9 squares 2⅝" x 2⅝" ▢ (A)
1 square 3" x 3" ⊠ (B)
(there will be 2 extra)
83 squares (D) 2¼" x 2¼"

Assorted Black Tone-on-Tones
16 squares 2⅝" x 2⅝" ▢ (A)
1 square 3" x 3" ⊠ (B)
56 squares (D) 2¼" x 2¼"
2 foundation patches

Assorted White Tone-on-Tones
9 squares 2⅝" x 2⅝" ▢ (A)
1 square 3" x 3" ⊠ (B)
(there will be 2 extra)
120 squares (D) 2¼" x 2¼"
2 foundation patches

Light Gray Tone-on-Tone
2 squares 2⅝" x 2⅝" ▢ (A)
2 squares (C) 2⅝" x 2⅝"
8 squares (D) 2¼" x 2¼"

Yellow Tone-on-Tone
for border #1
2 strips 2¼" x 37¼" for sides
2 strips 2¼" x 30¼" for top/bottom
6 strips 2¼" x 40" for binding
2 squares 2⅝" x 2⅝" ▢ (A)
4 squares (G) 5¾" x 5¾"

Medium Gray Tone-on-Tone
2 squares (C) 2⅝" x 2⅝"
2 squares (D) 2¼" x 2¼"

Light Blue Tone-on-Tone
36 squares 2⅝" x 2⅝" ▢ (A)
18 squares 3" x 3" ⊠ (B)
36 squares (C) 2⅝" x 2⅝"

White Tone-on-Tone
18 squares 3" x 3" ⊠ (B)
36 squares (C) 2⅝" x 2⅝"
18 squares (D) 2¼" x 2¼"

Medium Blue Tone-on-Tone
4 rectangles (E) 4" x 5¾"
18 rectangles (F) 2¼" x 5¾"

1 Making the Quilt Center

Referring to the unit diagrams, pair the A's in the appropriate colors to make unit 1's–5's as shown.

Unit 1
Make 16

Unit 2
Make 12

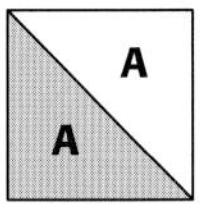

Unit 3
Make 2

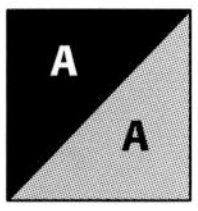

Unit 4
Make 4

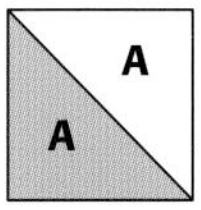

Unit 5
Make 2

Refer to the diagrams to make the unit 6, unit 7 and unit 8's.
Using the appropriate colors, first sew the B's together; join
to the A to complete the unit as shown.

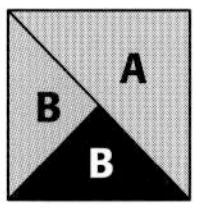

Unit 6
Make 1

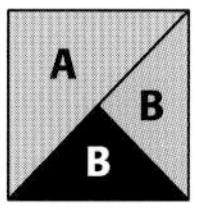

Unit 7
Make 1

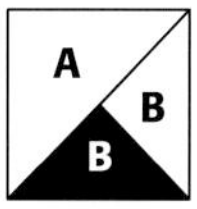

Unit 8
Make 2

Refer to the "Triangle-Squares" technique on page 57.
Pair the light gray C's with the medium gray C's to make 4
unit 9's as shown.

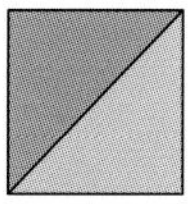

Unit 9 from C's
Make 4

Make a copy of the foundation and reversed foundation for the unit 10's. Foundation piece the units in numerical order, pressing and trimming after each patch addition.

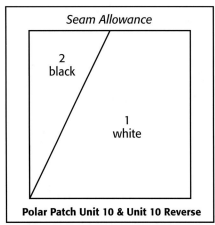

Seam Allowance

2
black

1
white

Polar Patch Unit 10 & Unit 10 Reverse

Patterns are the reverse of the finished block.
Pattern should measure 2¼" across including seam allowances.

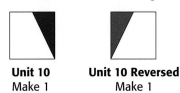

Unit 10
Make 1

Unit 10 Reversed
Make 1

Referring to the assembly diagram, join the D's and unit 1's–10's to make sections 1–6 as shown. Join the sections to make the quilt center.

2 Adding the Borders

Matching centers and ends, sew the border #1 side strips to the quilt. Repeat to add the border #1 top and bottom strips.

Refer to the "Triangle Squares" technique on page 57. Pair the white C's with the light blue C's to make 72 unit 11's as shown.

Unit 11 from C's
Make 72

To make a unit 12, sew a light blue B and a white B together; join to a light blue A as shown to complete the unit. Make 72 unit 12's.

B
A
B

Unit 12
Make 72

Quilting Placement

Join the units to a D patch as shown to make a block. Make 18 blocks.

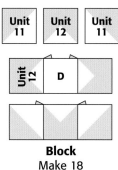

| Unit 11 | Unit 12 | Unit 11 |

| Unit 12 | D |

Block
Make 18

Refer to the assembly diagram. For each border #2 side strip, join 4 medium blue F's and 5 blocks as shown; add a medium blue E to each end. For each border #2 top and bottom strip, join 5 medium blue F's and 4 blocks as shown; add a yellow G to each end. Add border #2 in the same way as border #1.

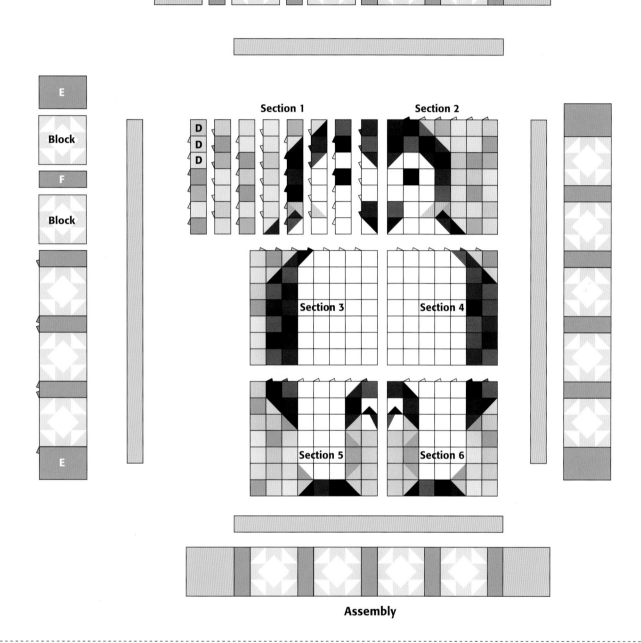

Assembly

---

3 Quilting and Finishing

Beginning in the upper left-hand corner of the background and using the patchwork as a guide, mark a grid over the background as shown. Layer and baste together the backing, batting and quilt top.

Quilt the penguin bodies, beaks, border #1 and blocks in border #2 in the ditch as shown. Quilt circles over the adult penguin's eyes and half circles over the baby penguin's eyes.

Quilt lines on the adult penguin's head, wings and feet as shown. Meander quilt on the white areas of the adult penguin's body. Quilt the marked grid. Quilt a looping line in border #1. Quilt the border #2 block design in the cornerstones (G) in border #2.

Bind the quilt. 🐾🐾

Jingle Patch

Santa's pal pays a holiday visit

Made by Peg Spradlin.

materials

Crib: 40¼" x 50¾"

Assorted Green Tone-on-Tones
1 yard *total* for background
Dark Brown Tone-on-Tone
¼ yard for the antlers and tree trunks
Medium Brown Tone-on-Tone
⅝ yard for reindeer
Medium Dark Brown Tone-on-Tone
scrap for ear and leg
White Tone-on-Tone
⅝ yard for reindeer and border #2
Black Tone-on-Tone
scrap for eye and hooves
Medium Green Tone-on-Tone
¾ yard for border #2
Red Tone-on-Tone
1 yard for nose, border #'s 1 and 2
and binding
Backing 2¾ yards (with careful basting, 1 fabric width at 1⅝ yards will be
sufficient)
Batting 45" x 59"

cutting

▱ = cut in half diagonally
⊠ = cut in half twice diagonally

Assorted Green Tone-on-Tones
12 squares 2⅝" x 2⅝" ▱ (A) (there
will be 1 extra)
1 square 3" x 3" ⊠ (B)
178 squares (C) 2¼" x 2¼"
Dark Brown Tone-on-Tone
8 squares 2⅝" x 2⅝" ▱ (A) (there
will be 1 extra)
24 squares (C) 2¼" x 2¼"
Medium Brown Tone-on-Tone
9 squares 2⅝" x 2⅝" ▱ (A)
2 squares 3" x 3" ⊠ (B) (there will
be 3 extra)
79 squares (C) 2¼" x 2¼"
Medium Dark Brown Tone-on-Tone
1 square 2⅝" x 2⅝" ▱ (A)
1 square 3" x 3" ⊠ (B) (there will be
2 extra)
5 squares (C) 2¼" x 2¼"
White Tone-on-Tone
9 squares 2⅝" x 2⅝" ▱ (A) (there
will be 1 extra)
4 squares 3" x 3" ⊠ (B) (there will
be 1 extra)
59 squares (C) 2¼" x 2¼"
14 squares (D) 2⅝" x 2⅝"

Black Tone-on-Tone
2 squares 2⅝" x 2⅝" ▱ (A)
1 square 3" x 3" ⊠ (B) (there will be
2 extra)
3 squares (C) 2¼" x 2¼"
Medium Green Tone-on-Tone
4 squares 3" x 3" ⊠ (B) (there will
be 2 extra)
14 squares (C) 2¼" x 2¼"
14 squares (D) 2⅝" x 2⅝"
10 squares (E) 5¾" x 5¾"
8 rectangles (F) 2¼" x 5¾"
Red Tone-on-Tone
for border #1
2 strips 2¼" x 37¼" for sides
2 strips 2¼" x 30¼" for top/bottom
6 strips 2¼" x 40" for binding
1 square (C) 2¼" x 2¼"
4 squares (E) 5¾" x 5¾"

1 Making the Quilt Center

Pair the A's in the appropriate colors to make the
unit 1's–7 as shown. (Note that units 4 and 7 use the
medium dark brown A's.)

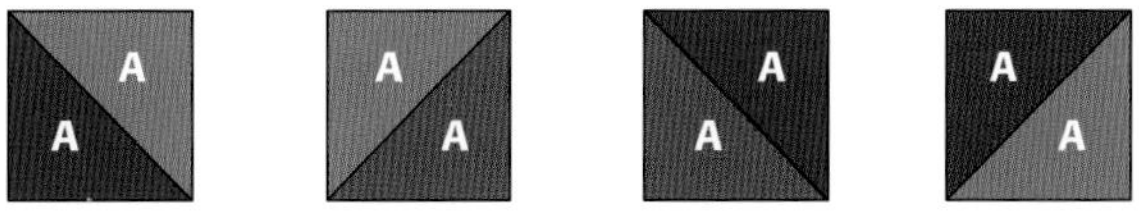

To make a unit 8, join a medium brown B and a black B;
join to a medium brown A as shown to complete the unit.
Make 2 unit 8's. In the same way, make units 9–13 in the
colors shown. (Note that a medium dark brown B is used in
units 9 and 10.)

Unit 1
Make 14

Unit 2
Make 7

Unit 3
Make 1

Unit 4
Make 1

Unit 5
Make 2

Unit 6
Make 3

Unit 7
Make 1

Unit 8
Make 2

Unit 9
Make 1

Unit 10
Make 1

Unit 11
Make 1

Unit 12
Make 1

Unit 13
Make 1

Refer to the assembly diagram; join the C's and units as shown to make sections 1–6. Sew the sections together to make the quilt center.

2 Adding the Borders

Matching centers and ends, sew the border #1 side strips to the quilt. Repeat to add the border #1 top and bottom strips.

To make a unit 14, join a medium green B and a white B; join to a white A as shown to complete the unit. Make 14 unit 14's.

Unit 14
Make 14

Refer to the "Triangle-Squares" technique on page 57; pair white D's with medium green D's to make 28 unit 15's.

Unit 15
Make 28

Join a unit 14, 2 unit 15's and patches as shown to make a block. Make 14 blocks.

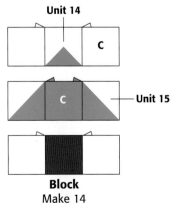

Block
Make 14

Refer to the assembly diagram. Noting the block orientations, join 4 blocks, 3 green E's and 2 green F's as shown to make

Quilting Placement

the border #2 side strips. Noting the block orientations, join 3 blocks, 2 green E's and 2 green F's as shown to make the border #2 top and bottom strips; add a red E to each end. Add border #2 in the same way as border #1.

3 Quilting and Finishing

Refer to the quilting diagram. Beginning in the upper left-hand corner of the background and using the patchwork as a guide, mark a grid over the background as shown. Layer and baste together the backing, batting and quilt top.

Quilt the reindeer, antlers, nose, ear, chest, hooves and border #1 in the ditch. Quilt the marked grid. Quilt a curve and a circle around the eye and a wavy line on the chest as shown. Meander quilt the head and body.

Quilt a looping line in border #1. Quilt curves in the trees of the border blocks connecting them with a loopy meander as shown.

Bind the quilt. 🐾🐾

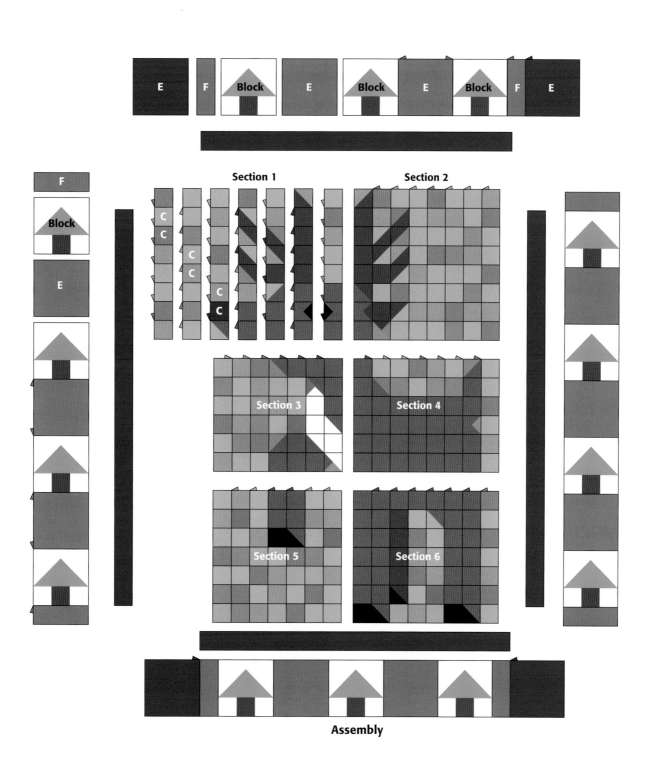

Assembly

Border Swap

When *Quiltmaker* introduced the **Patch Pals Collection**, we wanted these playful characters to be easy-to-piece and simply made from squares and a few triangles. The crib quilts in this collection are all the same size and their borders are interchangeable, making it easy to customize your project. These quilts make great baby or shower gifts for the special little one in your life.

For added inspiration, here are some border and color options to spark your creativity!

Quack Patch, page 16

Ruff Patch, page 4

Check out this ›
cheery duck with
a vibrant *Beary
Patch* border.

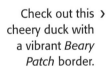

‹ You can customize *Ruff Patch* to match your favorite canine friend. This brown dog romps in the green grass using the border from *Quack Patch*.

Reader Gallery

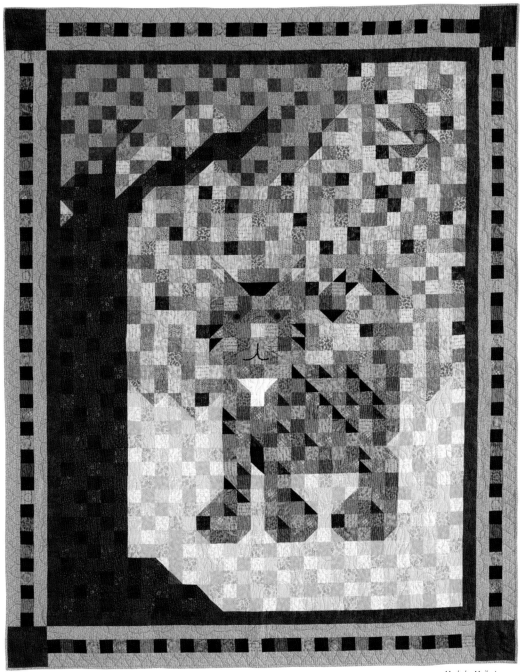

Made by Maila Josang.

Made by Robin Yokom.

Made by Lucy Rognes Bissell.

Made by Susan Courtney.

Made by Anne-Marie Bravo.

Made by Laura Nolletti.

Made by Bonnie Floyd.

Made by Tammy Goff.

Made by Jennifer Edmundson.

Made by Anne Morgan.

Made by Sky Masse.

Made by Mary Kennedy.

Made by Forest Jane.

Basic Lessons

techniques

Applique

The instructions give the applique technique used by the designer. Fusible applique patterns are already reversed. To convert between fusible designs and turned-edge, you may need to reverse the design. No turn-under allowances are given on applique patterns. When positioning patches, leave enough space around the outside edges of the block for trimming and seam allowance.

Finger crease the fabric in half lengthwise, crosswise and diagonally as needed to form guidelines for placement of the patches.

Use a tear-away stabilizer on the back to support machine stitching that is dense (like satin stitching) and to keep the fabric from tunneling. Choose a stabilizer that matches the weight of the fabric. After the applique is complete, gently remove the stabilizer.

Fusible Applique

Raw-edge applique using paper-backed fusible web is a fast and easy way to applique. Add ³⁄₁₆" underlap allowance to those edges that lie under another.

Trace the pattern pieces, also drawing the needed underlap allowances, on the paper side of fusible web leaving at least ½" between all the pieces. Cut about ³⁄₁₆" outside each drawn line.

To eliminate stiffness, try this variation for patches larger than 1": Cut out the center of the fusible web ¼" inside the drawn line, making a ring of fusible web.

Following the manufacturer's directions, iron the web, paper side up, to the wrong side of the fabric. Cut out the shape on the drawn line. Carefully pull away the paper backing. Fuse the patches to the background where marked.

To finish the raw edges, machine satin stitch with a colored thread, or zigzag or blanket stitch using matching or invisible thread.

Stitch-and-Flip

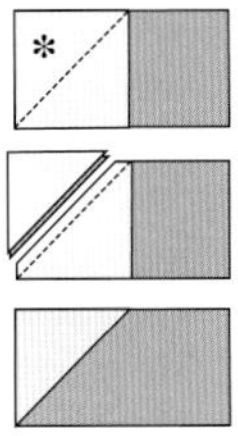

Align a patch (* in this example) on a corner of a unit or second patch right sides together. Mark a diagonal line on the * patch from corner to corner and sew on the marked line. Trim the seam allowance to ¼" as shown. Flip the patch open and press.

Fast Flying Geese

Align 2 small squares on opposite corners of the large square, right sides together. Draw a diagonal line as shown and then stitch ¼" out from both sides of the line. Cut apart on the marked line.

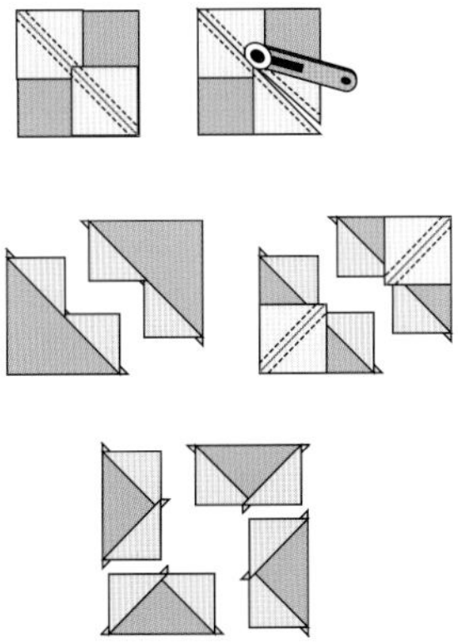

With the small squares on top, open out the small squares and press the unit. On the remaining corner of each of these units, align a small square. Draw a line from corner to corner and sew ¼" out on both sides of the line. Cut on the marked lines, open the small squares and press.

Each set of 1 large square and 4 small squares makes 4 Flying Geese. These units will finish at the correct size for each pattern. No trimming is needed.

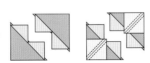

Triangle-Squares

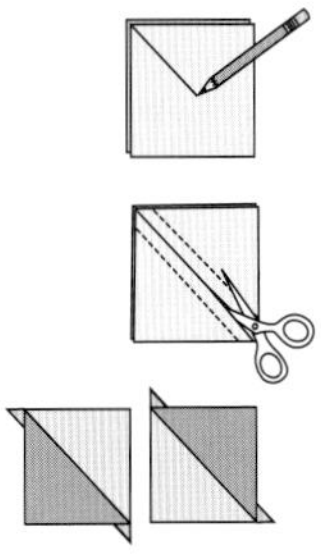

With right sides together and the lighter fabric on top, pair one square of each color that makes the unit. On the lighter patch, draw a diagonal line from corner to corner.

Stitch ¼" out from both sides of the line. Cut apart on the marked line. With the darker fabric up, open out the top patch and press the unit.

A pair of squares will yield 2 units. These units will finish at the correct size for each pattern. No trimming is needed.

Quarter-Square Triangles

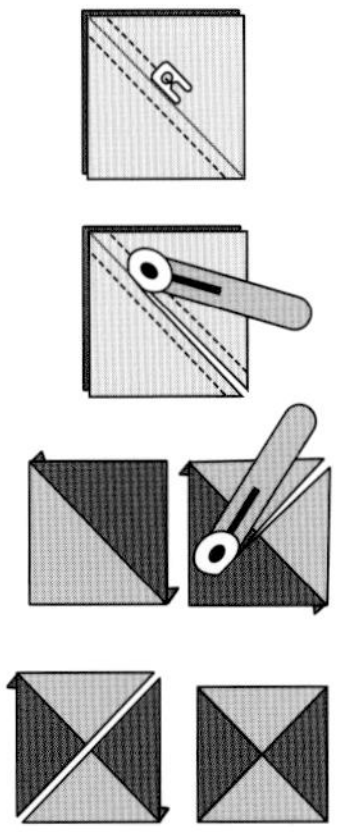

With right sides together and the lighter fabric on top, pair one square of each color that makes the unit. On the lighter patch, draw a diagonal line from corner to corner.

Stitch ¼" out from both sides of the line. Cut apart on the marked line to make 2 triangle-squares. With the darker fabric up, open out the top patch and press the unit.

Cut both triangle-squares in half diagonally as shown. Referring to the diagram, join the appropriate halves to make 2 units. These units will finish at the correct size for each pattern. No trimming is needed.

Foundation Piecing

Make paper copies of each foundation. Sew patches in numerical order. Center fabric under #1 extending beyond the seam allowances, wrong side of the fabric to the unprinted side of the paper, and pin in place from the paper side.

Turn fabric side up. Using a patch of fabric sufficient to cover #2 and its seam allowances, position the #2 patch right sides together on patch #1 as shown, so that the fabric's edge extends at least ¼" into the #2 area. Pin in place. Set a very short stitch length on your sewing machine (18–20 stitches per inch or 1.5 mm). Turn the assembly paper side up. Stitch through the paper and the fabric layers along the printed seam line, beginning and ending ¼" beyond the ends of the line.

Turn assembly to the fabric side. Trim the seam allowances to approximately ¼". Press the fabric open to cover #2 and seam allowances.

Repeat this process to complete the blocks or sections.

Use a rotary cutter and ruler to trim ¼" outside the seam line of the foundation, creating a seam allowance. Once all the seams around a foundation section have been sewn, remove the paper foundations.

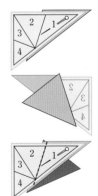

finishing techniques

Borders

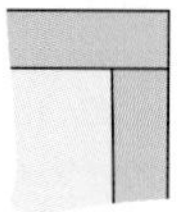

Squared borders are added first to the sides of the quilt center, then to the top and bottom. Lay the quilt top flat on a large table or the floor. Lay both border #1 side strips down the vertical center of the quilt top and smooth carefully into place. Slip a small cutting mat under the quilt top (you'll need to do this at the top and the bottom) and use a rotary cutter and ruler to trim the border strips to the same length as the quilt top. Matching centers and ends, sew the border side strips to the quilt. Gently press the seam allowances away from the quilt center. Repeat this process along the horizontal center of the quilt, including the newly added borders. Repeat for any remaining borders.

Marking

Trace the quilting motif on tracing paper. Place tracing paper under the quilt top with a light source behind. Lightly mark the design on the quilt top with a hard lead pencil or a marker of your choice. Test any marking product for removability before using it on your quilt.

Straight lines may be "marked" as you quilt by using masking tape that is pulled away after quilting along its edge.

Backing and Basting

Make the quilt backing 4"–8" larger than the quilt top. Remove the selvages to avoid puckers. Usually 2 or 3 lengths must be sewn together; press the seam allowances open. Place the backing wrong side up on a flat surface, stretch slightly and tape or pin in place. Smooth the batting over the backing. Center quilt top right side up on top of the batting. Pin the layers as necessary to secure them while basting.

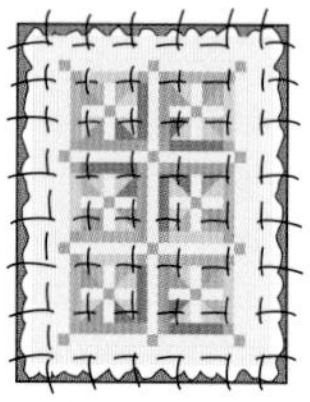

Basting for Machine Quilting

Tops to be machine quilted may be basted with rustproof safety pins. Begin at the center and place pins 3" to 4" apart, avoiding lines to be quilted.

Basting for Hand Quilting

Beginning in the center of the quilt, baste horizontal and vertical lines 4" to 6" apart.

Quilting

Quilt in the ditch refers to quilting right next to the seam line on the side without seam allowances. **Outline quilting** refers to quilting ¼" from the seam line. **Echo quilting** refers to quilting one or more lines of stitching in uniform distances away from a patch.

Machine Quilting

Before machine quilting, bring bobbin thread to the top of the quilt so it doesn't get caught as you quilt: lower presser foot, hold the top thread and take one stitch down and up, lift the presser foot to release the thread tension and tug on the top thread to draw a loop of the bobbin thread to the top of the quilt. Pull the bobbin thread to the top. Lower needle into the same hole created by the initial stitch, lower the presser foot, and start quilting. A walking foot is used for **straight-line** or **ditch** quilting. To **free-motion** quilt, drop (or cover) the feed dogs and use a darning foot. Start and end quilting lines with ¼" of very short stitches to secure.

Binding

Baste around the quilt ³⁄₁₆" from the edges. Trim the batting and backing ¼" beyond the edge of the quilt top.

To prepare the **binding strips,** place the ends of 2 binding strips perpendicular to each other, right sides together. Stitch diagonally and trim to ¼". In this way, join all the strips and press the seam allowances open.

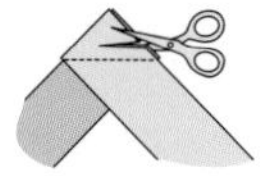

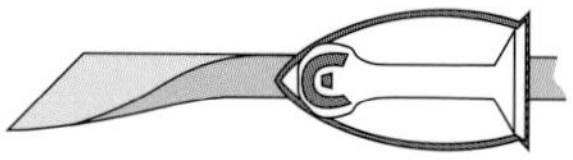

Cut the beginning of the binding strip at a 45° angle. Fold the binding strip in half along the length, wrong sides together, and press. Starting in the middle of a side and leaving a 6" tail of binding loose, align the raw edges of the binding with the edge of the quilt top. Begin sewing the binding to the quilt using a ¼" seam allowance. Stop ¼" from the first corner; backstitch. Remove the needle from the quilt and cut the threads.

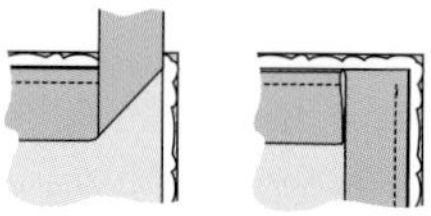

Fold the binding up, then back down even with edge of the quilt. Begin stitching ¼" from the binding fold, backstitch to secure and continue sewing. Repeat at all corners. When nearing the starting point, leave at least 12" of the quilt edge unbound and a 10" to 12" binding tail. Smooth the beginning tail over the ending tail. Following the cut edge of the beginning tail, draw a line on the ending tail at a 45° angle. To add a seam allowance, draw a cutting line ½" out from the first line; make sure it guides you to cut the binding tail ½" longer than the first line. Cut on this second line.

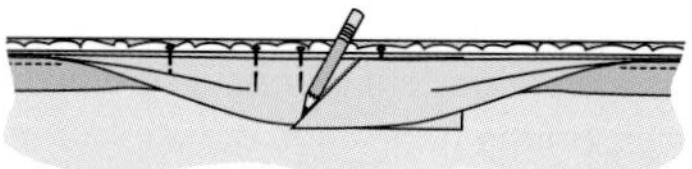

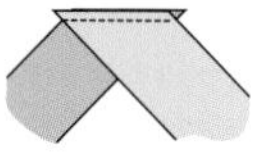

To join the ends, place them right sides together. Offset the points so the strips match ¼" in from the edge and sew. Press the seam allowances open. Press the section of binding in half and then finish sewing it to the quilt. Trim away excess backing and batting *in the corners only* to eliminate bulk.

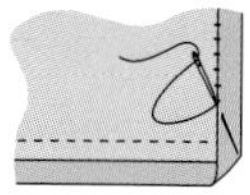

Fold the binding to the back of the quilt, enclosing the extra batting and backing. Blind stitch the binding fold to the backing, just covering the previous line of stitching.

Sleeve for Hanging

Sleeve edges can be caught in the seam when you sew the binding to the quilt. Cut and join enough 9"-wide strips of fabric to equal the width of the quilt. Hem the short ends of the sleeve by folding under ½", pressing, then folding and pressing once more; topstitch close to the edge of the hem. Fold the sleeve in half lengthwise, wrong sides together, matching raw edges.

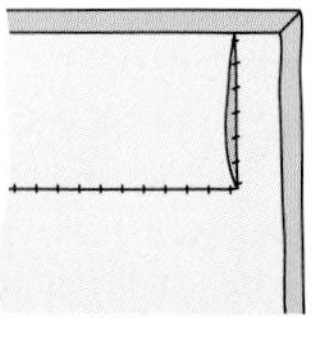

Center the sleeve on the back and top of the quilt and baste. Sew the binding to the quilt. Once the binding has been sewn, smooth the sleeve against the backing and blind stitch along the bottom and along the ends of the sleeve, catching some of the batting in the stitches.

Color Your Way

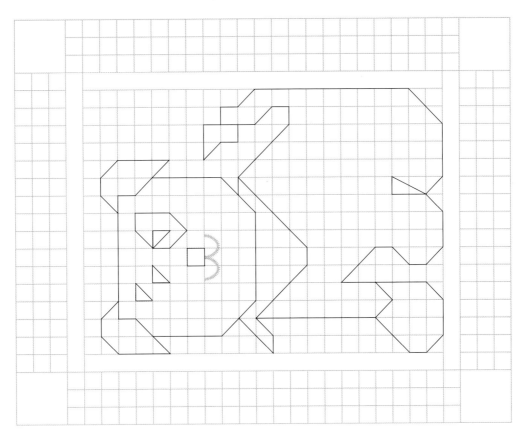

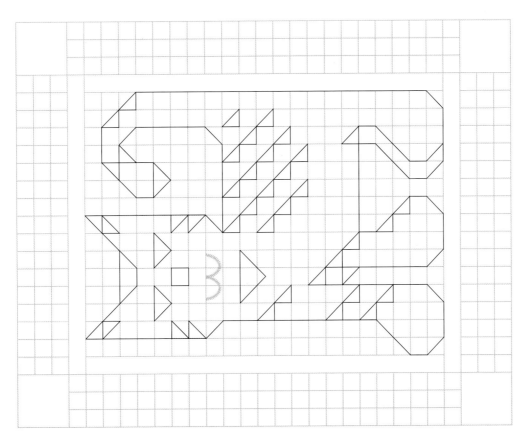

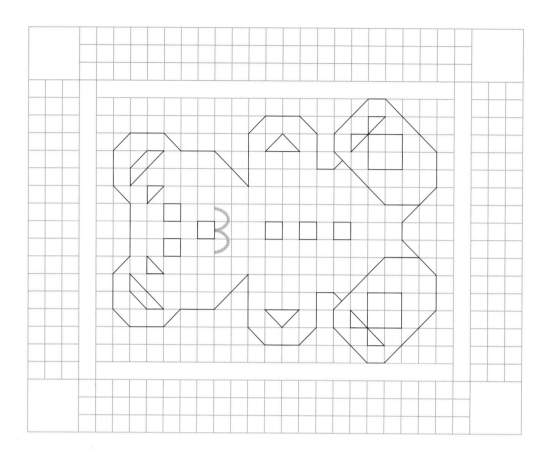

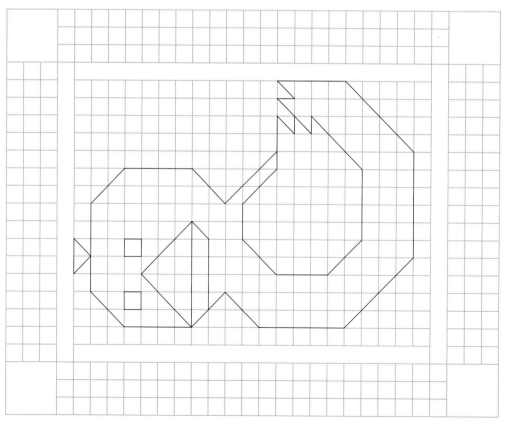

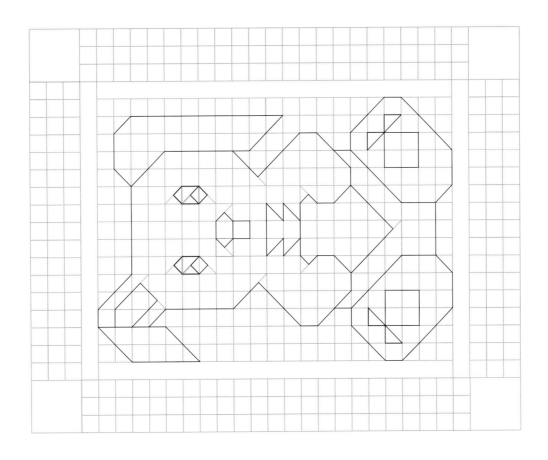

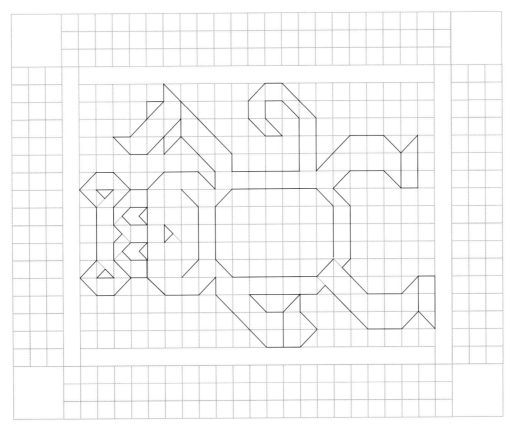

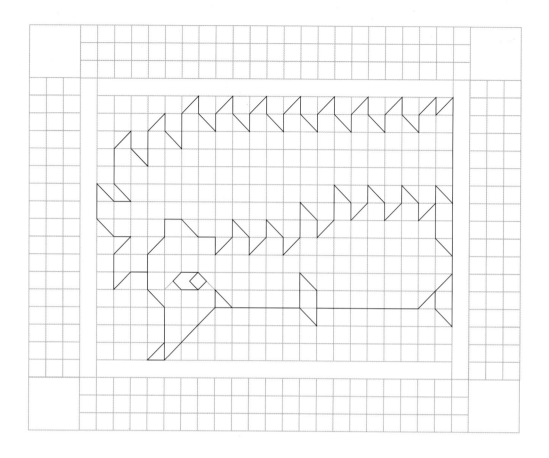

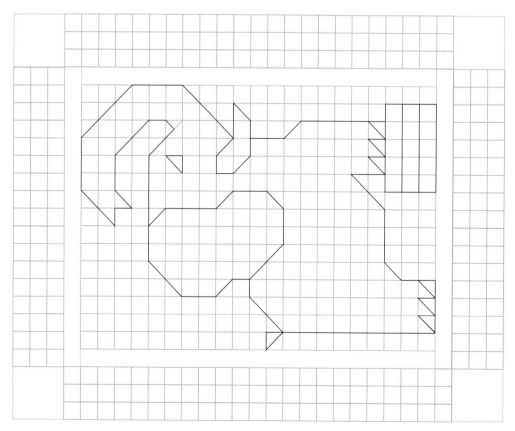

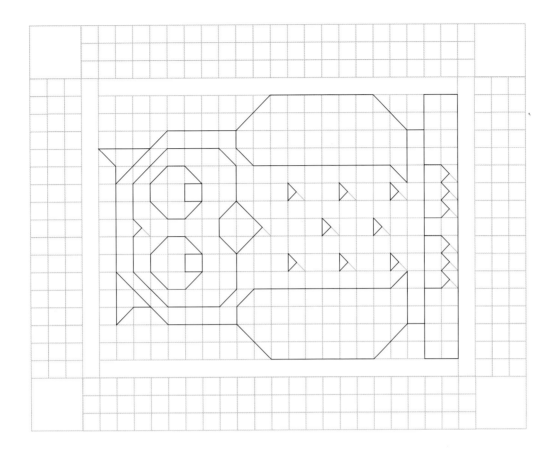

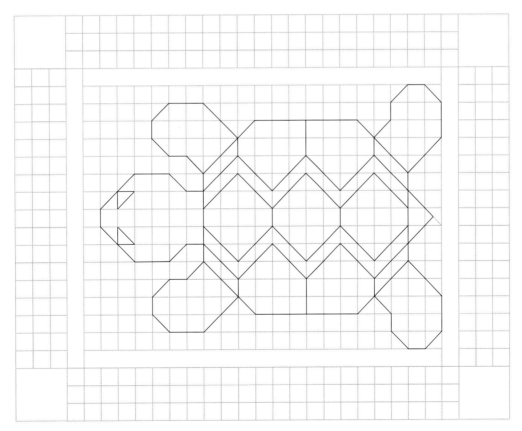

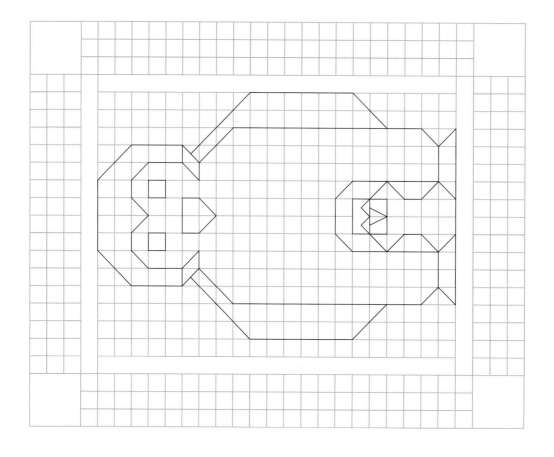

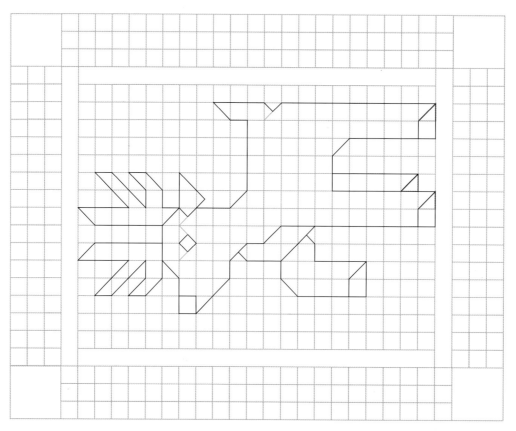